The Other Side of ZERO

"Debt Is Only Temporary"

Christopher L. Boyer

The Other Side of Zero: "Debt Is Only Temporary"

Christopher L. Boyer

www.theothersideofzero.com

Cover Layout Assistant: Anthony N. Baugh

Copyright © 2012 by Christopher L. Boyer

All rights reserved. No part of this publication may be reproduced, stored in a retrieval system, or transmitted, in any form or by any means, electronic, mechanical, photocopying, recording, or otherwise, without the prior written permission from the publisher.

ISBN-13:
978-1480173774

ISBN-10:
1480173770

"Even at birth we are in debt,
for we owe our mothers our lives."

For Mom! I love you with all my heart.

CONTENTS

	Preface	i
Chapter 1	What is "The Other Side of Zero?"	1
Chapter 2	Getting Started	10
Chapter 3	The System	32
Chapter 4	Money Saving Ideas	51
Chapter 5	Rags To Rags	71
Chapter 6	Ramblings About All Things Financial	74
Chapter 7	Doing It Together "Coupling Love And Finances"	98
Chapter 8	No "U" Turns	101
Chapter 9	Zero And Beyond	105

Bonus Excerpt

"The Ramblings of an Average Joe Stock Trader, 2nd Edition"   117
All the information I wish I knew in the beginning!

Bonus Excerpt

"Real Estate 101 Profit Max!!!"   131
101 Money Saving Ideas When Investing in Real Estate

Recommended Publications, Shows and Sites   139

"Jump In Now"   **142**
The Question To Answer Index

The Other Side of Zero

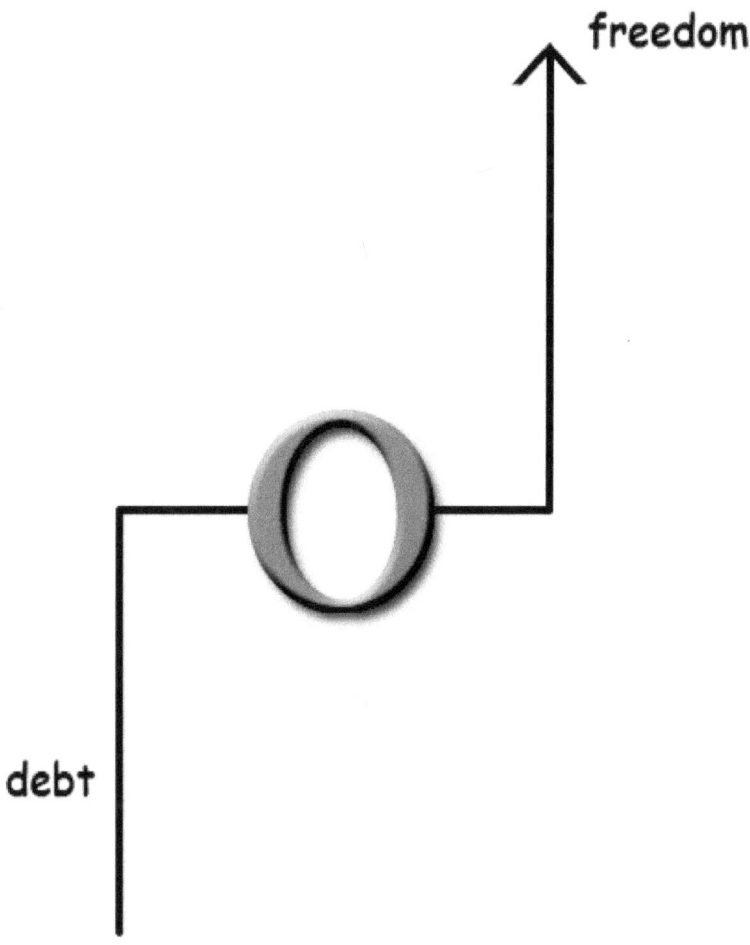

Christopher L. Boyer

PREFACE

The aging population was promised security. They were promised worry free retirement through the Social Security Insurance Administration, United States Government and through on the job pension programs. If you don't already know by now those systems are not working out for most people. People are reaching the age of retirement with nothing more than dwindling accounts, a small government check and more false hopes and promises that things are going to work out.

We were all once children. And for most of us we lived life without the worry of food, rent, insurance, and other expenses we just didn't have to worry about. Those concerns were left up for our parents to take care of. Then we grow up incurring monthly and annual expenses that gradually compounded into enormous amounts of debt. We will struggle our entire adult lives to try to achieve what we had as children.

As a child you had sense of security and your only concern was where to play today.

I want you to have that worry free sense of childlike enthusiasm again. I want you to wake up each day and explore the world around you without the stress of the cost of your life. I want to share with you the small things I have discovered in my life that makes life easy and stress free.

Financial stress and the worry of not being able to provide for your family is the number one concern for people of all generations. Doctors, medical reviews, even your mother will state the fact that stress kills. Keep living your life with the compounding never-ending stress and you won't have a life to live.

In the following chapters I am going to share with you a system, some ideas and basic concepts that if you choose to implement will change your financial life.

- No complex time consuming budgeting.
- No envelope system.
- No fifty-thirty-twenty plan.
- No more headaches and worries about money.

You will no longer need to be concerned with allocating funds to different accounts, putting enough money away for the bills coming due, a new car, or even retirement. All you need to do is spend less than five minutes one time on the simplest, easiest, financial plan you are ever going to experience. There is no system simpler than this!

According to figures from the US Census Bureau website 80 to 83 percent of all Americans are in debt.
www.census.gov

Knowing that…

"If you are going to do what everyone else is doing, then you are going to get the same results as everyone else."

Small legal info: I am not a financial planner. I am an average working class guy that uses this system every day. This system has afforded me a lifestyle that few get to experience and drives me to share this system with the world. Yes I have had ups and downs but this is the system I always fall back to because I know one thing,

IT WORKS!!!

I am not a certified public accountant and don't plan on being one. There are people in life that love to live accounting and those are the people you should consult prior to making any legal or investment decisions. This book is not a get rich quick book but if you utilize what's in this book you will be on the road to wealth in no time. How long it takes is up to you.

So to sum this section up; always consult a financial planner, accountant, tax advisor and attorney prior to making any investment or financial decisions.

This is the system that I use. When first trying to explain this system to another person I did not realize the extent of information that I had absorbed, developed and experienced throughout the years. When I first attempted to put this system into a book to share with others I ran into a few problems of stream lining the system. The book originally was filled with mathematical equations for the user to calculate using their own numbers. Many of the phrases and descriptions were so "alien" to most people not familiar with finance that I had to find a way to clarify everything for the everyday person. After review and multiple revisions I have simplified the system to the point in which this book works in unison with the website,

www.theothersideofzero.com

so you don't have to do the calculations. I am thankful I get the opportunity to share with you what I have learned.

What I have put in this book is the way you are going to get out of debt and build wealth.

With motivation, sacrifice, and drive you will be on the other side of zero.

The Other Side of
ZERO
"Debt Is Only Temporary"

Christopher L. Boyer

"Aim for wealthy and just enough is what you get along the way."

Chapter 1
"What is The Other Side of Zero?"

The other side of zero is where everyone in life struggles to be. It is where you no longer have to worry about bills and expenses. It is a place that is very similar to where most people were when they were children.

Growing up you did not worry about day to day issues such as electricity and water bills, car payments, mortgages, rent, health insurance, buying food and working long hours. Growing up you awoke each morning to a new day of adventure and play. Growing up you just lived life.

Like the old saying goes, "You had time to stop and smell the roses."

As a child you had the time to explore and experience life worry free. This system is going to allow you the opportunity to experience that freedom and sense of security once again. This simple, quick, wakeup call, is going to change your life forever. What you are about to learn in the following chapters is,

1. There is no need for complex systems, budgets and headaches.
2. There is no need to continuously struggle for something that one small change now will give you later in life.

Why does debt feel like its draining everything out of you in life? Why does debt not feel so bad when you are creating it?

Think about this,

Let's imagine that you have free cash each month of about two hundred and fifty dollars. You don't have any upcoming bills so you decide to buy a car with a payment of $250 per month. You know you can handle the payment, additional insurance, and maintenance and you are really excited about the new car.

As time passes the thrill of the purchase is wearing off and the new car smell is gone. Now the car is just a car that costs you $250 per month.

How much does a $250 monthly payment impact your life?

You would think if you owe $250 per month then the impact is only $250, right?

Wrong.

Instead of having a positive $250 per month that you could spend on anything, including other expenses or investments, you now have a negative $250 per month. If you imagined the purchase on a scale it would look something like this,

Free cash per month=

+$250

Car payment per month=

-$250

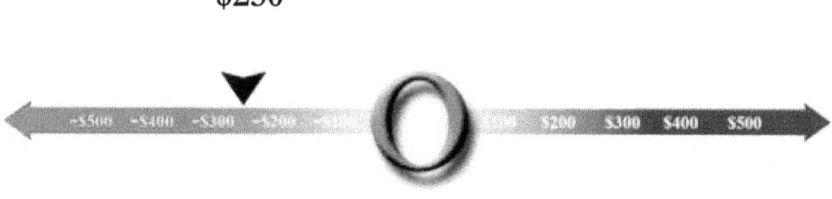

Financial impact on your life is the difference between your earnings and your expenses.

-$250 ← difference → $250 = $500

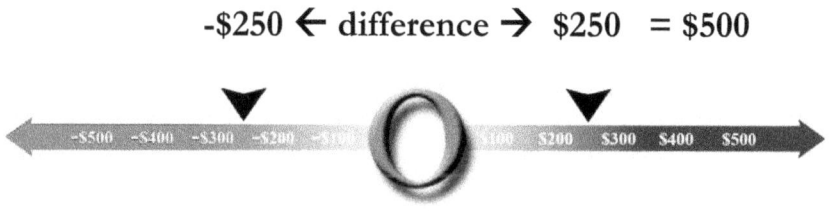

A $250 per month payment actually impacts your life by $500. How can that be?

Instead of being plus $250 per month you are now actually negative $250 per month. That is a $500 swing in the opposite direction. You are not actually spending an extra $250 per month but the financial and emotional impact it has on your life is equal to $500 per month. Instead of being able to purchase an extra $250 per month of stuff or make investments, you can't, the cash is already tied up in a debt.

> ***NOTE*** If it's a depreciating asset like the car example above then the money tied up in the asset is gradually growing down, which increases the impact on your life. Instead of spending a long-term total of $15,000 at the end of your loan your car is only worth $4,000. The same thing occurs if you were spending $1000 per month on a house mortgage. The impact the $1000 has on your life is $2000. The good thing with a house mortgage is, in the long run you should be able to cash out by selling your house and getting most of your investment back if not more.

Haven't you ever wondered why when you pay off a long standing monthly bill you feel so free, like an enormous weight is lifted off your shoulders?

Paying off debt lets your accounts start to explode upwards away from zero and allows your mind to be free from the monthly reminders of having things due. (Until you find your next monthly purchase to drag you back down again)

The feeling you have when you are completely debt free is amazing, but so many people have been in debt for so long that they don't remember what it feels like.

Once the never ending cycle of accumulating debt starts it is extremely difficult to stop. And at this point you have only two options,

1. Win the lottery.
2. Make a change.

Since the odds of the first one are one in approximately seventy-six million your only real choice is the second.

This book is not just about getting out of debt it is more importantly about building wealth. In order to be wealthy we must first deal with the debt. After taking care of the debt we will then use the same system we learned and apply it to building huge amounts of wealth. It's that simple!

So what is zero, and why is it important?

Zero is the crossover number from negative to positive or positive to negative.

Any amount that is negative to zero is an expense or debt.

Any amount that is positive to zero is income or wealth.

The difference between the two is the impact.

Zero is the one point that defines you making it financially for the month or not. Zero is the minimum that you make each month to cover the maximum amount of expenses you have per month. For some of us getting to zero each month is a never-ending struggle that never seems to end. You think to yourself that if you can make it to payday then everything will be ok. Then payday comes and you feel good for maybe a day or two, if you're lucky. Then the feeling of not having enough begins to creep back into your mind and your happiness starts to fade back into the cloud of worry and concern.

- Are you living pay check to pay check?
- Do you find yourself struggling at the end of every month?
- At the end of the year do you find yourself maxing out your credit cards to buy Christmas gifts, praying you'll get tax money to pay off the lines of Christmas credit?
- How are you going to change this viscous cycle?
- How are you going to take charge of your financial life?
- Do you want to be wealthy?
- Do you really want to live the life you have always wanted?

This system works on all time frames whether it is a day, month, year, or a lifetime. This system is for everyone and is not contingent on age, income level or how you got into debt. People can build debt over a long time or jump into it with one quick purchase. Unanticipated medical costs or a surprise divorce could have left you with enormous amounts of debt. How you got the debt does not matter, debt is debt. You will use what's in this book to fix your life.

In this book we are first going to give you some basic principles that will assist you while working this system. Many of these suggestions are simple to implement and typically go overlooked in the busy chaos of daily life.

Next we will review some topics that will help you understand where some of your money is going.

Then we will use the website to do the calculations to create a basic starting point of where you are right now.

We will use this starting point as a "Zero" point to determine how making small, simple changes will affect your long-term financial health.

After we have established your "Zero" point and have addressed simple changes we will visit other financial topics that will help open your eyes to different ideas typically not thought about. These ideas are to be used in conjunction with the system to help maximize MONEY IN and decrease MONEY OUT.

We will get into more details about zero and the magic of this number in upcoming chapters.

Don't worry this book is not filled with complex mathematical calculations that you must be a mathematical wizard to figure out. I have simplified the system to the point that all you will have to do is go to the free companion website

www.theothersideofzero.com

and answer a few simple questions. The website was created to be easy to understand, accessible on multiple browsers, operating systems, mobile devices and most importantly it is user friendly. The site uses JavaScript to perform calculations and advanced features. JavaScript is a programming language that works with your browser to make sites more interactive and user friendly. Most modern browsers have JavaScript built-in so there should be no problem accessing the site. If you have any issues be sure that you have JavaScript enabled on your browser. You will know if your browser does not have JavaScript enabled when you first get to the site. At the top of the screen it will say,

"This is a JavaScript site. Your browser does not have JavaScript enabled. Click for instructions on enabling JavaScript."

If you do not see the above statement, JavaScript is ready to go and there is nothing for you to do except use the site.

If you have any issues accessing or using the site please feel free to check the FAQs page for frequently asked questions or contact us anytime. On the main page of the site you will find a link to all of our contact information.

One more note about the website.

We do not record or use any information about what you input, and we do not share any of your information to third parties or subsidiaries.

This book, and the companion website were solely created to help you better your financial life.

Chapter 2
Getting Started

We are going to get to the main system but first we want you to know a few simple things. If you want to jump straight to the system, go ahead and jump to Chapter 3, but some of the information I am about to share will help you understand the system better.

> Stop, take this book and go to your car. Slightly adjust your seat so the back sits a little straighter and raise the bottom seat height so you can see a little better. Leave your seat at this new position. I will share with you later in the book why you just changed your seat position.
>
> (Don't forget to adjust your mirrors to account for the new seat position.)

Most people are in debt and financially upside down. Right now the United States economy is doing terrible, the stock markets down, and millions of people are losing their jobs and their homes. Finding work for the majority of college graduates and veteran workers is extremely difficult and the older you are the more challenging it is. So will this system still work?

You don't have to work at McDonalds to be rich!

This system works for everyone in any type of situation. Age, gender, and race will have no influence on your success. For this system to work there is one thing you must have above all else and that is <u>income</u>. You must have money coming in. It does not matter the type of job, or how much you get paid You just have to have money coming in. The reason why you have to have money coming in is because we need to establish a financial baseline to measure all of your actions off of. If you have no income you have no baseline.

If you are not currently employed the skills in this book will still assist you but the system needs income to work. Many community employment offices have counselors available for assistance with job education, skill improvement and job placement. I encourage you to use the free services provided by your community.

Does it matter if I only get paid minimum wage?

No, the amount you get paid does not matter. Anyone can build use this system, get out of debt and build massive amounts of wealth. It is not the amount you get paid that is a concern; it is the amount you actually keep that is. Higher pay does speed the wealth building process up and so does spending less. If you can't get more pay per hour than you need to spend less.

Extra note about a job:

A job is great but two is better than one. If you have the time and drive do something extra. Having a higher paying job does make building wealth easier but anyone can build wealth no matter your income. Keep a steady paying job as your primary income provider and dabble in side jobs until you find your secondary niche. When I was thirteen I mowed and raked lawns, washed cars, and cleaned horse stables until I could save up enough money to move on to doing something else. When I was roughly twenty I bought my first house. In life when I stumble, get crazy, and spend a chunk of money, I go back to what I started with, working hard. The point is doing what you know now until you get to where you want to be. Then when you are financially stable, start exploring your other interests in life. If your exploration of other career paths and interests knocks you back down, don't be discouraged, gracefully get up and try again. The great part about this system is it is structured to always work. This system doesn't change as you change. This system is always there to provide for you when you go astray and you can do it over and over again.

Get used to the idea that,

> ➢ **You will blow your money!**
> ➢ **You will make a big stupid purchase!**
> ➢ **You will think, "I can," when you should be saying, "I really shouldn't."**

We all go through the same phases and we all respond to those phases similarly. The key is to learn from each phase and move on.

One summer when I was a kid, my family went to Six Flags just outside Atlanta, Georgia. My Dad and I were at the top of the ride called the "Free Fall." I looked over at him and he had his eyes wide open. I said to him, "Why do you have your eyes open, are you not scared?" he responded with, "The fear is the fun!" With the exception of my lovely wife and the excitement of getting married, throughout my entire life I have always had more fun trying to achieve something then actually having it.

The fun is in the fear of trying!

The point is any job is better than no job. Any source of income will provide you with some sense of security. Yes it may be a job paying well below what you're used to, and what you feel your worth, but that is just the way it is for right now. Sometimes in life you just do what you have to do, but you never give up.

Most fast food locations are always hiring. Temporary job services always have something for you to do based off your skills. If you're out of work call a local pizza delivery chain they are always hiring drivers and inside help. I guarantee you will be surprised at how much above minimum wage you can make per hour delivering pizzas. Depending on the region of the United States you are in; check the local real estate investment clubs for help wanted. The investors typically are looking for labor and people with general knowledge for making repairs. I know these are not the greatest jobs but remember something is better than nothing and somewhere is always a good place to start. People say, "It is easier to find a job if you have a job."

So what was step one?

Get any amount of income by doing any legal job necessary.

Step 2

I discourage you from calculating how long it will take you to become debt free!

Calculating how long it is going to take to pay off your debt is discouraging and extremely depressing. How long it takes you to pay off everything and become debt free is going to change as you wipe out each debt and become more motivated and driven to be debt free and wealthy. Once you begin seeing your money churning and rolling into itself, you will be driven to work harder to get more results. It is like a dangling carrot in front of a work horse. The horse can't get the carrot but tries and tries with all its might. You are the horse and the carrot is being debt free and wealthy. So giddy up!

> As your mindset, current situation, and bank accounts change, so too will the length of time to get to the positive side of zero.

Stick to the plan we are going to lay out. Do not deviate from the plan. Trust me, you will want too. You will see things that you want to buy and now that you think you have a little money in your account, will start seeing everything on blue light special. Fight the urges to buy and find something else to occupy your mind. The urge and want created when you have money is powerful and difficult to resist. In times of desperate need of want (not need) I would suggest buying something small as a gift to someone in need. This way you fulfilled your urge to buy and you helped out someone else.

So many people want to be debt free

So many people are confused at how they got themselves into this debt to begin with. Those same people charge there fuel fill ups and morning coffee to their most warn out card in their purse or wallet. Many people will start this journey to debt freedom. Motivated and driven to being debt free they start turning off light switches and skipping lunch. Then after a few days they see something they got to have and say to themselves "I have been good the last few days so I should reward myself." They then proceed to charge it. I wrote this book to help keep you focused.

Many people start down this debt free path without the proper structure in place and then become overwhelmed, discouraged, lose track and give up. This book is here to help motivate you and keep you on track. Work the plan and allow the small changes to take effect. The long term rewards are going to be amazing and worth the wait.

I say to you, "Take things one step at a time and lets deal with the here and now."

"Focus on debt and you get more debt." There is a great section about money in the book, "The Secret" by Rhonda Byrne. If you have not read this bestselling book you should get it now. It is one of my listed recommended readings at the end of this book.

Open your eyes to where you are in life financially right now. Then say to yourself, "This is unacceptable," and move on. Don't get hung up on your past. Realize that what has occurred in your past is your past. Learn from your mistakes and do what you can to prevent those actions from occurring again. I have complete faith that if you stick to this plan, your tomorrows will start changing for the better.

Read this book, use the system and,

- ✓ You will be able to afford those things in life you have always dreamed of.

- ✓ You will be able to put your children through college without worry.

- ✓ You will be able to finally live life.

Things to Note

All numbers we will be referring to are calculated on a nine to five, forty hour work week basis. It does not matter if this is your schedule or if the total number of hours you work is equal to forty or less. This system works for all people no matter your profession or the number of hours a week you work. This system even works for the "self-employed."

The reason we use a nine to five and a forty hour work week to calculate with is to establish a simple starting baseline for all people to measure themselves against. If all people on the earth each used a different length stick to measure one foot then who would know how long one foot is?

We will cover this more in Chapter 3, "The System."

The first thing you need to "KNOW"

Each dollar you put away above zero is actually changing your life, though initially the change is so minute that it may go unnoticed. As you add to those dollars the change will become more evident. Your accounts will now say you can afford it. Your brain will say "yes I can." Even your heart will say "I can help." But the reality is you still can't. You need to build a strong foundation so those unexpected expenses don't wipe you out and put you back on the other side of zero. Be patient and keep yourself distracted and busy. Your wealth will only appear to be growing slow in the beginning, don't get discouraged. Remember implementing your new actions will be evident in your life before you know it.

The second thing you should "KNOW"

—Everyone wants

While working through this system you may tell yourself that you don't want to live without things and luxuries in life. The reality is you are already living without. Think of all the additional opportunities you would have if you weren't in debt and had money. Have you ever heard it takes money to make money? Money provides additional opportunities to make more money. Think of it like this, "Would you be able to afford a fifty thousand dollar house if you didn't have the ten percent required to put down as a deposit?"

Most people think about what they are going to spend their money on instead of thinking about what they can buy that will make enough money to buy the item that they wanted.

An added bonus to having money is it allows you to be able to change your mind set to think "What am I going to do?" (Help a neighbor in need, pay off a strangers medical bills anonymously, send your parents on a cruise, and pay for a random person's lunch in a restaurant)

> The most fun you will ever have in life is giving what you have worked so hard to obtain away!

The first thing you should "DO"

—Stop Going Shopping

This is one of the most difficult things for people to stop doing. Our technological society bombards us with continuous advertisements for products and services we typically don't need.

Google scans our emails looking for key words to suggest page advertisements to us.

Watching television programs we get small ads in the corner of the screen to solicit products and shows, so we can watch more commercials and advertisements.

Every item we own that has a name or logo stamped on it is an advertisement for more of that product.

The best marketing campaigns are the ones so sophisticated that you don't notice them occurring. Everywhere you go, and everything you see is an advertisement.

Simply put, stop shopping. If you don't know what is on sale, or available for sale, you will not convince yourself that you need to buy it.

Estimating the amount being paid in and paid out

It is a good rule of thumb to always calculate more money owed out than received in.

For example,

Let's say I have a car payment of $263.55 per month. I will typically round it up to say $275.00. This rounding up makes quick calculations much easier and leaves a little extra room for errors or surprise expenses.

If I am expecting a paycheck to be $583.52, I will round down the amount I think I will get to about $550.00.

> **Remember round up the amounts you owe out, and round down the amounts you are owed in!**

Why do you have a savings account?

Most people have a checking and a savings account. Most people have the money they use most often in the checking and a little bit of what they think is "extra money" (see section on "extra money") in their savings. But the reality is they don't typically have more than a few days or weeks of savings in the account. Most banks only pay interest on the balance if it is over a specified amount, and the interest is so low it's not worth the risk of overdraft fees in another account because it was short. The banks convince us that opening a savings is a good way for us to put money away. The truth is the savings is for the bank, not you. They don't want you to withdraw your money frequently because they loan the money (your money) out to other people. The interest they collect from the other person is what they then give you a small percentage of, interest. They can't make secure loans to people if they don't have locked in, guaranteed funds that they can loan out. Why do you think they penalize you for making more withdraws per month from your savings then one or two?

Most people don't carry the minimum specified amount in their savings from month to month, so my question is, "Why have a savings account at all?" Simplify your life. Stop trying to convince yourself that you're saving because you have a savings account. Keeping track of numerous accounts is pointless. If someone gave you one hundred dollars would you go to the bank and open up two checking accounts and a savings account splitting the one hundred dollars between all three accounts? No, they would place the hundred in one account thinking it's not really enough to be split up. So if someone gave you one thousand dollars, would you split that up? Most people will say "yes." But why?

The amount of money being considered "a lot" is only the perception of the one who has the money. To a millionaire there would be no reason to split up the thousand dollars because it is somewhat equivalent to the one hundred dollars for the average person.

Banks will tell you the reason people should have a separate savings is that most people will want to spend money if they can easily get ahold of it. If you can't stop spending your money than it does not matter what account you are pulling it from. The question you should ask yourself then is, "why am I always spending all my money?"

Wealthy people do not have savings accounts; they have money market and brokerage accounts. Why would you spend time earning a nickel when you can just as easily be earning a dime?

My thinking about savings?

It's all savings. Every dollar you make is money that you're trying to keep. If you think classifying some of your money as "savings" will prevent you from spending it I will say this to you,

Most people when growing up, or with their own children, like to put little marks on the door casings of their house to measure their height at various ages. It's fun to see how tall you grow, or see how much your child has grown over a period of time. Why not do the same thing with your money? Take your money put it in an account and watch it grow. Separating money amongst multiple accounts makes it seem like less and takes the fun out of watching it magnify and get big. Real big. There are only a few times you should need to separate the bulk of your cash.

1. When you exceed the maximum insurable value by the institution holding your money.
2. When you move some of the money into different diversified investments for protection and higher rates of return.
3. When you get the craving to buy something big that will not give you a return on your money. Examples include automobiles, trips, big Christmas gifts and birthday gifts for others, etc.

The point is just like with kids, "feed your account, and watch it grow."

Another point about savings,

People like the idea of the word "SAVINGS." It makes them feel comfortable as if they have something that will be there to help them in a tight situation. Let me ask you this,

- Does it make more sense to spread your money amongst multiple accounts so that one account may be at risk of having an overdraft penalty or a low funds charge at months end?
- Are you really getting something in return for having your money split amongst multiple accounts at your bank?

If your bank charges you fees for accessing your own money or if your bank charges fees for withdrawing more than once or twice per month, it's time to switch banks!

Why are you paying to keep your money in someone else's shoebox?

Banks are other people's shoeboxes that charge you to store your own money in them. If your bank is charging you any fees find another shoebox. Credit unions typically have no fees on standard accounts. Banks are businesses. There whole purpose is to make money. Banks convince you it's safer to have your money in a bank. Banks convince you there credit card is safer than cash. Banks convince you that you should use checks. But let me ask you this, what happens when you lose a fifty dollar bill? What happens when you lose your check book? What happens if you lose your credit card and don't alert the bank quick enough?

Lose the fifty and only be out fifty. Lose the credit card and if someone uses it be out fifty and some headaches to fix the problem. Lose the check book and your nightmare could last weeks or even years.

Remember the bank always has a hidden motivation.

> **You should never pay to have someone else hold your money.
> They should always be paying you!**

Extra Money

When you owe a business or someone money there is no "EXTRA" money!

The whole idea of extra is completely absurd. The average person will never have extra money. Extra money is what we call a reason or justification to being able to purchase something. Extra money is an excuse to do something.

If you think of life on a small scale, yes extra money is defined by the Oxford English Dictionary as, "more than usual." But think of life looking at the big picture and,

You will make a certain amount in your entire lifetime. You will spend a certain amount in your entire lifetime.

If you make more money in your entire lifetime than you will spend, then, and only then, will you have, "more than usual."

Another way of putting it:

Have you ever thought?

"Oh, I have this unexpected fifty dollars so I can afford this music album or new pair of shoes."

"Oh, I get my tax return check in about a month so I will use that to pay off this purchase I am putting on my credit card."

The fifty dollars you unexpectedly received is not extra money. If you owe anyone, any amount you must pay them first because that fifty belongs to them.

Imagine you have no car payment, no cell bill, no rent due, and no credit card payments due, is the money now considered extra money?

NO, it is not extra money!

Why is it not extra money?

Next month you will have another round of expenses to be paid out. Another mortgage payment, another water bill, another electric bill, etc.

So is it possible to ever not have a payment and have extra money?

YES!

Extra money is the amount of money you have in excess of all the money you owe out over your life span. In order to figure this number out calculate all money you will <u>ever</u> owe and get that amount of money. Get one dollar above that and "bam" you have extra money.

Are you thinking?

"How do you predict all life expenses, aren't there things called unexpected surprises?"

Yes there are unexpected surprises. But when creating a well thought-out plan you have to take into account unforeseen scenarios.

How can we account for unforeseen scenarios in life?

By reviewing other people's lives you can estimate expenses related to certain activities that may present themselves in your life. There are very few people on this earth that have stepped outside the boundaries of normal and revolutionized society. And since I am betting you and I have not stepped outside the box yet, we can learn from those people's experiences. The book entitled, "The Millionaire Next Door," written by Thomas Stanley and William Danko is a great place to start researching lives of average people that aren't so average when it comes to money.

Find people with money and do what they do. If you don't know anyone with money personally, start at your local library. Everyone knows librarians are loaded… with information on books that share the life stories of highly successful people. Some great names to start your research on can be found on the "Forbes Top 100 List" or in any edition of, "People" magazine.

I thought we would not have to create a budget or time consuming plan?

We don't. Once you read and understand the next chapter you will understand better.

What about TAX return money?

Tax return checks are not extra money. In most cases it is your own money being given back to you with no interest being paid on it. You have given the United States government an interest free loan. You should be paying the taxes on the money you make, but you shouldn't be getting money back at the end of the year. The amount you pay to the government each check should be the amount you owe, not excess. Consult your employer or a licensed tax specialist/advisor about correcting your paper work so you have more of your own money available to you now and you get less back at the end of the year.

Another odd idea people have about paying taxes is,

"If I make more money than wont I have to pay higher taxes?"

Of course you will be paying higher taxes, that is just common sense. But what most people don't pay attention to is the **"MAKING MORE MONEY"** part of their ridiculous statement.

I would love to be paying the IRS one million dollars a year in taxes. Do you know why?

If I am making enough money that I have to pay one million dollars in taxes a year than my annual income is far greater than one million a year. Having to pay more taxes is just an excuse people use to justify why they are not making more money.

A zero situation for you to think about

If you owe five hundred dollars today on your credit card and I gave you five hundred dollars to put into your bank account how much money do you have?

ZERO, Nada, Nothing, Zip!

I have asked this question to many "just average people" and I have been surprised at how many have responded with, "I have five hundred dollars."

You have nothing. You owe someone else the five hundred dollars.

How much money do you have tomorrow if you didn't use the five hundred dollars?

NEGATIVE ZERO, because you owe interest on your borrowed five hundred dollars.

When it comes to debt and paying interest remember this,

"Today you are worth nothing, tomorrow you are worth less than nothing, and each day going forward you become even more worthless."

Harsh isn't it! But that is reality.

There are two main types of interest. Interest you do not want and interest you do want.

Interest on credit cards, mortgage payments, auto loans, school loans, etc. is the interest you don't want.

Interest on cash (or equivalent securities paying you) is the interest you do want.

Too bad the interest you typically get from banks for having money is less than the interest you have to pay to the banks when you borrow money.

We will address more about the two types of interest later in this book, but for now you only need to know that there are two types one good and one bad, and the bad one is the one you need to avoid at all costs.

Good interest on your money is the easiest way to get your money to grow.

And that now brings us to two simple questions,

1. How much do you spend in a day?
2. How much do you make in a day?

Chapter 3
The System

I have developed this system to make it easy for you to see the results in the future of your financial actions, today.

A Brief Summary

Go to the website, answer a few questions about your current financial situation, and get results. It is that simple! If you have already been to the website you have already done this, but you were probably left with a few unanswered questions.

- What do the numbers on the results page mean?
- Why are these numbers so important?
- How can I use these numbers to change my life?

In this chapter we are going to answer these questions and many more.

First we are going to go through the simple process of using the site. Throughout the instructions we will note the importance of each section and why each number is an important key to your success.

Then we will conclude the website section by explaining what the numbers mean and how you can make small adjustments that will change your life.

A Brief Summary of the Calculations

We are going to calculate what you make on average per day, and then we will calculate how much you spend on average per day. The difference between what you make and what you spend should be a positive number.

If your numbers are negative then you are what we call, "bleeding," which is spending more money than you are making, and you are in an extremely critical situation and need to make immediate adjustments to your income and expenditures.

If your total amount per day number is a positive number then we will focus on how much it is positive and what ways can we make it more positive.

The difference between what you make per day and spend per day we are going to call your "spread." The more distance between your expense amount and your income amount the better off you are financially in the long run.

By using these numbers we are going to calculate how much you should be saving per day, per month, per year, and finally the amount you will have at retirement.

One item to note, for the purpose of establishing a starting point baseline we calculate what you make on **AVERAGE** per day. I know that you don't make money on a day you don't work but you still have to balance this amount. For example: If I spend $50 per day in average expenses and I make $60 per day and only work five days a week, the extra ten dollars per day for all five work days goes to cover the expenses on the days I am off. As you see in this scenario I will only have enough to cover one of my days off.

A second example: You spend on average $80 per day in expenses. You work five days a week and your take home pay per day is $120. The first two days of the work week the money you make over $80 (expenses) goes towards your day off expenses. So at the end of your fourth work day you have made enough money to cover the expenses on the two days you are not working. You should be clearing at the end of a seven day period, if you don't spend one dollar above what's stated, forty dollars.

> Make more money in a day then what you spend in a day. Follow this simple rule and you are on your way to the other side of zero.

Let's get started,

Use the companion website that was created for this book to do the math for you. Just follow the instructions and input what you can in the boxes.

If you have not already been to the website go there now

www.theothersideofzero.com.

Press the large green start button on the home page.

Choose between "I am single," or "I have a partner."

Click the "I have a partner," button if married or you are with a companion that participates financially in life with you.

NOTE FOR COUPLES

All expenses asked to be inputted will be your <u>combined</u> expenses. The rest of the site will be self-explanatory.

Next choose "Expenses Form" (blue button).

NOTE If you already know your EXACT monthly expenses you can skip this by pressing skip. I highly recommend not skipping the expense form. If you take just a few minutes and fill out each expense item to get the final monthly expense total it will make the final calculation on the next page much more accurate. As you will soon see, a missed thirty dollar amount can add multiple years to your end results (more about years in a moment).

This is a simple expense form to help you visually remember all your expenses and then gives you a total at the bottom. On the expense form fill out each monthly expense that you have. If you do not have each bill in front of you estimate.

***Remember always round up for money owed out.

Not all areas will apply to everyone, so fill out what you can and leave blank, or enter 0 (zero), in the boxes that don't apply to you.

Use the additional "Miscellaneous" boxes, and the "Other" boxes to list any additional expenses not listed on the form.

NOTE For expenses that you have only once a year divide the expense amount by twelve to get your monthly amount, and input that number.

If you make a payment twice a year, divide that payment by six and input that number.

When you have finished putting in your totals press the "Calculate" button.

The amount shown is your total monthly expenses.

NOTE If you see the letters NAN in the input field after you click on the calculate button you inputted something incorrectly. You may have inputted a letter or character instead of a number. Check your numbers.

Write down this total monthly expense number, we will be using it shortly.

Print this from now by pressing the print button. If you are viewing this site on a mobile device and don't have print capabilities make sure you write down the total monthly expense amount, you will need that amount on the next page.

Click the "Next" button. (green with arrow)

You are now on the **"Check Your Financial Health"** page.

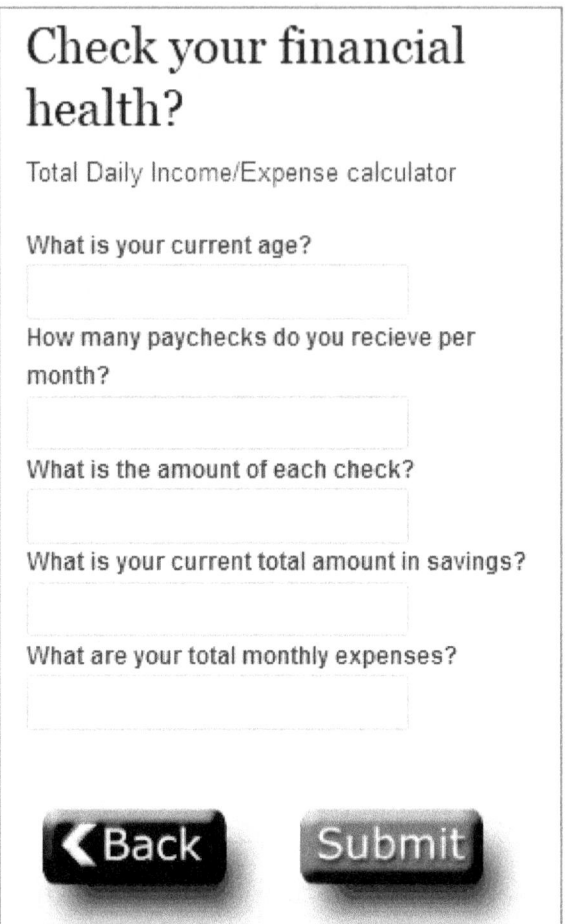

On the "Check Your Financial Health" page there are five things you need to input,

1. Your age?
2. How many checks do you get per month?
3. How much is your check <u>after</u> taxes?
4. What are your current total savings?
   (Including IRA, 401K, stocks, bonds, mutual funds, etc.)
5. What are your monthly expenses?

NOTE FOR COUPLES

Your page has inputs for two people.

You will be entering the age, number of paychecks, and amount of paychecks for each person.

The expenses will be your combined monthly expenses.

Enter your age.

Enter the number of checks you get per month. If self-employed or you receive several checks with different amounts or you receive cash of various amounts enter one (1) in this box.

> We will consider checks to be any sources of income. This varies from person to person. Some people receive four checks per month, some only two. Some people receive checks and cash throughout the month. Some people only receive cash. This system works for everyone, as long as you have income.

Enter the amount of each check. Enter the after tax income but before deductions amount.

If you receive various forms of income such as cash and checks, add your monthly income up and enter the amount into the box.

Enter your total current savings. This is the total of all money you have currently saved including but not limited to your IRA, 401K, mutual funds, CD's, savings accounts, stocks, bonds, cash, loose change, etc. If you have zero savings enter 0 (zero) or skip this box. If you are doing this as a couple enter your combined savings amount.

Enter your total monthly expenses. If you skipped the expense form input the total of all your monthly expenses.

NOTE For expenses that you have only once a year divide the expense amount by twelve to get your monthly amount, and input that number.

If you make a payment twice a year, divide that payment by six and input that number.

Make sure to include everything you spend per month. The more accurate your monthly expenses are the more accurate your results will be. If you need to go back to the expense form go there now.

Now click "Submit"

Your financial results now appear on the page. **Print this page now.**

Your results,

- The average income per day is the amount you make every day based off your income. We spread your pay across all days, those worked and those not worked for the purpose of establishing your current day rate.

- The amount you spend per day is your average expenses broken down into a day by day cost. This amount is what you spend every day whether you are out at the movies or sitting home on the couch. This number is based off your total monthly expenses if you inputted all of them.

- The amount you should be saving per day is the difference between the amount you make per day minus the amount you spend per day. This number should be positive. If not positive, in the next chapter we will give you some ideas on how to improve this number.

➢ The amount you should be saving per month is the amount of free cash you should be banking per day totaled up based off your current financial situation. If this is low or negative, we will show you in the next chapter some ways to increase this amount. This is the amount most people at months end are short. This is the number that most people can't figure out where their money went. It is easy to spend money day to day and not be conscious of the long term totals. Then surprisingly at the end of the month we ask, "Where did my money go?"

➢ The next line is the amount of money you should be saving annually based off your current financial situation. This amount is contingent on you not spending one more dime other than what you inputted for your expenses. This amount does not take into account any additional sources of income not stated, simple or compounding interest. (we will get to that in a moment)

- The amount you should have at retirement is based off all of your savings minus all of your expenses till you are 65 then adjusted for inflation. What does this mean? Simply put this is the amount of money you will have at the age of 65 if you continue making the exact same amount as when you filled out the form, and you do not spend one more dollar other than what is stated on the expense line. Meaning,

YOU DON'T DO ANYTHING ELSE IN LIFE OUTSIDE OF WHAT YOU CURRENTLY ARE DOING!

- The next line tells you the number of months and approximate years you will have enough savings for after the age of 65. This is the amount that if you were to stop working at 65 you would than live off of. If this number is negative than this is the number of years you subtract from the age of 65, meaning, you will go broke before the age of 65 unless you change your financial life.

As each year passes your money is worth less, this is called inflation. Your money twenty years from now will be worth less than what it is today. Groceries will cost more at the store. Gas will be more expensive. Your rent will be higher. We accounted for this adjustment by using a historical average rate of inflation and applied it to the monthly expenses to determine what your money will be worth in the future. We could also apply inflation to your savings that you don't have and we could try to estimate you getting a better job but those things are not consistent and unknown. What we do know is that the money you make in the future will be worth less, and the money you spend on expenses will be more.

By creating the results page we have established a baseline. This is your starting point.

How is this my starting point?

By knowing these numbers we can adjust them, which in turn adjusts your future. Let me show you how,

Make sure you printed the page out or wrote down all the numbers. This is very important!

Now **reset** the form.

If your previous answers are still not displayed in the input boxes take a moment and fill out the form again, but this time subtract $50 from your expenses.

Click submit.

Look at the number of years you have now added to your financial life after the age of 65. That is only a $50 a month savings. That small amount just added **(your number here)** to your life. How awesome is that! You can now see how saving a dollar will impact your life in the future.

There are only two ways to improve your financial life.

1. Increase your income.
2. Decrease your expenses.

And now we have provided you with a tool that allows you to see real results.

All you have to do is adjust your monthly expenses down, or your income up, to get the exact number of years you plan on living work free in the future.

Another example:

Reset the form.

Increase your income on the income line by $20 and decrease your expenses by $50.

Click submit.

That is amazing isn't it? If you increase your pay per check by just $20 and decrease your monthly expenses by $50, (which could be as simple as not eating out or buying a months' worth of coffee at Starbucks) you would add **your number here** years of money worry free living to your life.

Simple adjustments to the Income and Expense boxes allow you to see end results without having to play "wait and see."

Play around with increasing and decreasing your income and expenses. You will see that making small changes can have huge impacts on your end numbers and your life.

Now that you can see the true results of your saving and spending all you have to do is implement simple changes to either to get results.

Simply put,

You have to make more money in one day then you spend in one day! By focusing on what you spend on a day by day basis you can make adjustments in real time to the numbers at the end of your life. Don't buy a coffee and a donut once a week and **"BAM"** an extra year of not worrying about money.

In the next chapter I am going to show you some typical expenses people have in life and how much of a financial impact those expenses have on their lives.

NOTE If any of the numbers on the results page are negative (example: $ -250.00) you need to seriously sit down and start incorporating the ideas in this book into your life. (More about negative in later in book)

Notes and Some Frequently Asked Questions?

Why do we use after tax income?

You do not actually make your hourly rate of pay. That number is just a creative way of blurring the line between your fairy tale life and reality. What you actually make is what makes an actual real impact on your day to day life. If I say to you I am going to pay you one hundred dollars an hour but then say I am going to keep 50% of that to help others and another 30% for new roads how much do you actually make? Twenty dollars an hour, so why then do you tell people you make one hundred dollars an hour.

How do you calculate what you spend per day?

You spend money every day, whether you sitting at home doing nothing or out shopping. The days you don't work and the days you do, you spend. Each person has life expenses. For some those life expenses are much higher than others. To reduce these expenses you must first find out how much you're spending per day. To do this make an itemized list of all your monthly expenses (examples of monthly expenses include automobile payment, electric bill, rent or mortgage, etc.). Then make a list of all your annual expenses. Divide your annual expenses by twelve (examples of annual expenses are automobile registration, house taxes, home insurance, etc.).

Why when I enter my income and expenses does the final results end up negative even though my annual savings is showing a positive number?

Awesome question. The results are inflation adjusted on the expenses. This would be similar to saving an amount of money per month and then compounding the interest on that amount monthly. The final result is showing negative because the amount you currently make twenty years from now is worth less than what it is actually worth today. If you make $12 hour now that same $12 twenty years from now will not buy you the same amount of stuff: It will buy you less because stuff will cost more AND your money will be worth less.

Why did you not adjust for inflation on savings?

There is no need. We formulated a base for you to measure all income and expenses off of. The point in this is to determine what you need to be doing. After you discovered where you are financially you will make the necessary adjustments to maximize your interest earned. There is no way for us to calculate what investments you will make and what rate of return you will get. One of the few facts we have to work with is the historical rate of inflation which typically is two to three percent.

What is a "Wash Event" or "Wash"?

A "wash event" or "wash" for short, is when one item balances out another item. For example, if you were budgeting an expense of $80 per month for a water bill but did not yet have the bill, you are estimating what you think the bill would be. Then say you estimate your electric bill to be $100 per month. The water bill comes in and is only $60, below your estimate, and the electric bill comes in and is $120, which is over your estimated budget. The extra money you didn't spend on the water bill then covers the surprise expense of the higher electric bill. Hence the two expenses create a "wash." The two expenses balanced themselves.

Another "Wash" example:

Thirty years ago the national minimum wage was $3.35 per hour (http://www.infoplease.com/ipa/A0774473.html). As the years passed the minimum wage increased but so did the expenses of the average individual. People are now making more per hour but now have additional expenses such as cell phones and internet that are practically required in today's world. So, though it appears you are making more, you are actually making less. The increase in pay is washed flat by the new expenses of life.

More frequently asked questions are listed and answered on the website www.theothersideofzero.com under the FAQs link.

Chapter 4
Money Saving Ideas

You don't know where you're going unless you know where you are at. In the previous chapter titled "The System," you used the website tools to discover where you are currently at financially. Now in this chapter we are going to list ways you can decrease your expenses on everyday things.

Take time to do just one of these items and you will cut your monthly expenses considerably.

These ideas are to help you stimulate the creative side of your brain and think of ideas that help you conserve the money you currently have. All these ideas will not apply to everyone and may not work in all situations. Take from this list what you find useful and share it with others. Make your own lists and keep them readily available for frequent review.

1. Don't drive around looking for the cheapest gas price. There are simple to use free phone apps that help you locate the cheapest gas in town. Another tip is to check the oil futures on your phone at www.cnbc.com . If the oil futures closed up for the day go ahead and fill your car up today. If the oil futures closed lower on the day, wait till tomorrow to fill your car up with fuel.

> Driving around for cheap gas lifelong total cost =
> **$ 4,152.90***

2. Don't waste your time putting just a couple of dollars in fuel in your automobile. Go ahead and fill the vehicle up with gas. You will save more money in the long run filling all the way up then you will burning fuel going to the gas station every couple of days to put a few dollars more in your tank.

3. Go to a community college for the first couple of years instead of a paying the high four year institution tuition.

4. Don't go to a for-profit school for higher education. For-profit schools are in the business of making money for their shareholders. They lack in motivation to educate you, and have the drive to bleed you for every dollar including the money the government gives you in grants and loans.

5. Choose a hobby that makes you money instead of costing you money.

> $25 a month hobby
> lifelong cost =
> **$ 20,764.47***

6. Use coupons. It only takes a few seconds of checking online to find a coupon for about anything. Spend a little time and save a few bucks. But don't spend huge amounts of money buying a bunch of products just because it's on sale or you have a coupon. Sales and coupons are what you should be looking for if you have to buy something, they shouldn't be an excuse for buying. I am sure you have said to yourself or another this phrase,

> "It was on sale," or "I had a coupon."

If you weren't going to buy the product did you actually save anything? No, you actually saved nothing and you spent money that could have been used for something else.

7. Don't buy used tires. Used tires will wear out quicker putting you in a situation where you are replacing them more often.

8. Don't order food for delivery.

Instead of having paying to have food delivered, spend the few minutes and pick it up. The delivery cost restaurants apply to your ticket is sometimes more than fifteen percent of your meal. The driver delivering your food doesn't get this money as a tip. They typically only pay a dollar to the driver for fuel.

9. Limit your eating out at restaurants.

This is one of the highest lifelong expenses most people will incur. When I was growing up going out to a restaurant or ordering pizza delivered was a luxury that was saved for special occasions. The joy and excitement of going out is lost when you eat out frequently. Save going out for special occasions.

> Eating out
> lifelong cost =
> $ 137,045.52*

10. Turn your water heater off, or put it on a timer so it's not continuously heating water when it's not in use. Only turn it on prior to needing it. This is one of the biggest wastes of electricity a home owner has.

In most apartments the water heater is electric and can easily be switched off and on at the breaker panel.

How long does it take for the water heater to heat up?

It normally takes a smaller water heater about 20 minutes to reheat. It takes about 35 minutes for the taller water heaters to reheat.

The water in the tank if used normally (daily) will stay hot. You do not immediately run out of hot water if the electric water heater is turned off. The tank still has hot water in it for many hours.

If you rent where you live, talk to your landlord about installing a timer on the water heater.

11. Don't go window shopping.

Many people like to go to the mall or local electronic store. Many people browse for things online. **Stop!** If you don't know what is for sale then you won't convince yourself you need to buy it.

12. Turn down your thermostat. Who doesn't want a nice crisp house to come home to after work, but is the cool air making you feel good while you're at work?

Put your AC on a timer to regulate the temperatures when you're not at home. Also look into investing in attic insulation or thermal windows. Most energy spent in the home is lost through poorly insulated walls, ceilings, floors, windows, doorways, and poorly insulated duct lines.

Consult a home inspector to do an evaluation of your house to see where you are losing the most energy.

"A 10-degree drop can knock as much as 15 percent off your utility bills."

http://money.cnn.com/2005/06/02/pf/smartest_real_estate_0507/index.htm

> 15% Lower thermostat
> lifelong savings =
> $ 37,376.05*

13. Refinance your home. Consult a licensed mortgage specialist to review your current interest rates and payoff schedule. A small investment now can really add up the savings over the life of the loan.

14. Mobile homes are depreciating assets. This means they go down in value similar to automobiles. I worked for an appraiser that would not appraise a mobile home for more than one hundred thousand dollars. To him there was no possible justification for going over that amount (other than the value of the land attached to the mobile home). If you're not buying a mobile home park, or a mobile home as a rental investment, stay away.

15. Have a garage sale. Go through all the things you have and get rid of all those things you don't need. Clutter free clean space just feels better allowing you think better while putting some of your lost cash back in your pocket.

> Bag of chips a week
> lifelong cost =
> $ 9,966.95*

16. Make a list before you go grocery shopping. Most people go to the grocery store thinking they only need milk and bread and then leave the store with bags filled with groceries. Making a list helps you stay focused and purchase only what you came there for. One three dollar bag of chips a week adds up to an extra $144 a year, and who needs the extra calories?

17. When you have to buy something always check www.amazon.com first. You will be amazed at how many products they have available for fantastic prices compared to brick and mortar stores. Be cautious, while you're searching for your item, don't browse. Browsing sparks ideas of want. Want then turns to need, and need then turns into more spent money!

18. I once dated a girl which refused to get a doggie bag when leaving a restaurant. Don't throw tomorrow's lunch away. There is no shame in asking for a to-go box. Leftovers make great next day meals.

19. Use grocery store bags as trash bags. Pretty simple savings. Why would you buy bags to throw away?

20. Do business with a credit union that has no fees. Banks charge fees because they are in the business of making money. At credit unions you are a shareholder, so you are entitled to payment for your shares. (Some minimum balances may apply, check with your local credit union)

> Lifetime of a bank
> $5.00 a month fees =
> **$ 4,152.89***

21. Disconnect your home landline phone. Who needs a home phone anyway, when you have a "YOU" phone in your pocket!

> Landline phone
> lifelong cost =
> **$ 24,917.37***

22. If you don't mind giving up a lot of your time cash in the car and start using public transit. Use the time standing around waiting for the bus or trolley listening to audiobooks on your MP3 player or read a book. Want to go farther start riding a bike to work or school but remember to get health insurance first. A small fender bender with an uninsured motorist can quickly give you a financial and literal headache.

23. There is a lot to be said about negotiating, and you really can save a ton of money when purchasing, but to me there is a fine line between negotiating and just being a "jackass." I have ran into so many people in life that the first thing out of their mouth is, "will you take less?" or "what are you going to give me?" Anyone that has ever listed anything for sale on Craigslist knows what I am talking about.

24. Pawn shops are good places to pick up items, or so they tell me. I don't really like the whole idea of a pawn shop. The show on television is great but the actual business idea of giving people practically nothing while they are desperate is not my style. Getting a reasonable discount is ok but pawn shops typically just take advantage of people. The other issue I have with pawn shops is they typically deal with merchandise that has been stolen. I know that police are cracking down on stolen goods and pawns shops, but if you want to reduce theft and home break-ins then society should reduce the number of pawn shops, or impose stricter policies and increase enforcement of those policies. Have you ever had your lawn mower or your tools stolen from your garage or your construction site? Why do you think there are so many tools for sale at pawn shops? In life I would rather pay a little more for something I know is honest then get a "good" deal at a pawnshop.

25. Ask for a raise. All they can do is say "No." There are many books written about the subject so do some research on the best way of asking before you ask.

26. Watch television on your computer and give up the expensive cable connection. Many of the most popular television shows are available online for free.

> Cable lifelong cost =
> $ 45,681.84*

27. If you're going out with friends, designate a driver and then drink at home before you go out. It is easy to spend fifty to a couple hundred dollars out drinking with friends in a single night.

28. Change all your light bulbs to energy efficient bulbs. These bulbs cost a little more but in the long run they will more than pay for themselves. They typically need to be replaced less often and the glass is thicker so it makes moving them to a new home pretty easy. I have been moving from house to house my first set of energy saving fluorescent bulbs for about eight years. I have had one break and only one burn out so far. I had a family member who bought a new house; the first thing we did was go through the entire house inside and out, and replace all the light bulbs. We replaced ninety-two light bulbs. I was amazed at how many bulbs were in that house.

How many bulbs are in your house? Stop now and go count them, you might be surprised.

I have found the best place to get the energy saving light bulbs is at big bulk wholesale stores like Costco, Sam's Club an BJ's.

29. Frequently check your automobiles tire pressure and air filter. These two items can greatly reduce fuel efficiency. This cost, though not really noticeable unless you track your fuel usage over a long period of time, can really add up over the life of your automobile.

30. Exercise at your local park or at home instead of paying gym memberships. See also tip number 45.

> Gym membership
> lifelong cost =
> $ 29,070.26*

31. Many communities have free events for the public. Where I live every Tuesday at a local park they have free admission to residents, to many of the museums, gardens, and exhibits.

32. Get an annual pass to the zoo. Not only does your money help support animal healthcare and research but who doesn't love going to the zoo. An annual pass is typically not much more than the cost of a one day pass. A zoo is a great cheap way of entertaining yourself and your children.

33. Carpool with a neighbor or find an online site that helps link like-minded carpoolers up.

34. Shut off all unused circuit breakers in your breaker panel or put your individual electronics and appliances on timers.

35. After washing allow your clothes to air dry instead of using the dryer.

36. Something fun to try:

Many of you have probably heard George Noory on Coast to Coast AM. If not, it's a late night radio show that is heard around the globe. The shows website is www.coasttocoastam.com . Mr. Noory has a frequent celebrity numerologist on the show named Glynis McCants. Her website is www.numberslady.com. During one of the shows she mentioned writing the number eight on a sheet of paper and putting it in your wallet. She stated, "In numerology the number eight encourages financial security and prosperity."

After hearing the show I put an eight in my wallet and my life financially since has been fantastic!

I don't know if the eight had anything to do with it, or if the continuous thought of the eight each time I opened my wallet made me more conscious of money, but I now have nothing to complain about.

I kept losing the piece of paper so I permanently had the number affixed to me exactly where my wallet would go. Now I am not recommending permanently affixing the number eight to your body but I would recommend putting the number eight in your wallet.

Glynis McCants states, "You are simply letting the universe know that you are ready for more financial prosperity in your life."

37. Put the "frequently most forgotten to shut off light switches" in your house on motion sensors. A small investment in the motion sensor switch can save you a sizable penny in the long run.

38. Use the library internet connection to check mail and do research. Most libraries have a limited amount of time per user so plan ahead and don't input vital personal information.

39. Drink tap or filtered tap water instead of buying expensive bottle water. Or buy your bottled water in gallon size or five gallon size containers.

40. Reduce your monthly cell phone bill to the minimum plan needed. Your cell phone should be for emergencies and business. Unlimited plans can be found for as little as fifty dollars a month. Unlimited talk and text can be found for only thirty-five dollars a month. Check out www.cricket.com. Why should you be paying more?

> Additional cell phone services
> lifelong cost =
> **$ 29,900.84***

41. Though you're not at the point in which you should be taking a vacation, when you do or if you must travel here's a tip!

When making travel plans check out the travel section of the Costco website. There deals match or beat that of other online discount travel brokers <u>and</u> typically offer Costco members additional benefits such as rental cars, room upgrades, spa treatments, and discounted excursions. For example I went on a trip with my wife to the Big Island of Hawaii. The Orbitz ticket price for airfare and Marriott hotel stay for 7 days was $2,795.70. The Costco package price was the exact same but it also gave us a rental car for the entire week, and full buffet breakfasts at the hotel we were staying at. The full breakfast buffet price per person was eighteen dollars a day not including tax and gratuity. There were two of us, so the total food savings on the week was approximately $252.00. www.costcotravel.com

42. Costco, BJ's and Sam's Club

Saving money at a big time wholesaler is a great way to stretch your funds. Wholesalers typically have discounted prices ranging from 15-25% lower than chain grocery stores and save you quite a bit of money overtime. The catch is the majority of shoppers at these wholesalers spend more money by purchasing items they wouldn't typically purchase or buy an abundance of single items that they will not ever use.

When shopping at wholesalers always prepare a list of items before you go, and stick to the list. They make it real easy to get distracted and buy more.

Some of the best items to save money on at wholesalers are laundry detergents, shave gels, hair products, body soaps, toothpaste, and razors. When buying these items in bulk you maximize your savings because they typically never expire or have an extremely long shelf life.

43. Whenever possible always use cash for all transactions. Most people when using credit cards spend more. They typically disconnect from the purchase as if it's not real money. When the monthly statement comes they then feel it was like real money, but only for the minimum amount owed that month.

44. If you have a bunch of loose change around your house or in your car, but don't want to take the time to roll it to cash it in at the bank, count out only enough to be just shy of a full roll and deposit that. They can't force you to roll your change if there isn't enough of one type of currency for a full roll. I typically do this when I deposit a check or deposit cash. Though on a number of occasions, I have only deposited $.49. I will admit the person behind the counter does give you an odd look at first, but after a while when your account balances start exceeding theirs those odd looks turn into questions about opening higher interest rate accounts.

45. If you love sports and various hobbies enroll in your local community college or trade school. These schools offer classes like tennis, golf, swimming, basketball, football, soccer, weightlifting and many others. For just the cost of one time school admission and the cost of the class you will be getting in shape and earning college credits.

<u>Example 1</u>

If you like going to the gym two to three times per week, enroll in an aerobics class or weightlifting. Not only is it much cheaper than an annual membership you get your very own personal trainer (the teacher).

<u>Example 2</u>

If you like going to the driving range and improving your golf swing then take a golf class. The class fee is going to be the credit hour cost plus a one-time driving range fee. When enrolled they provide you with clubs, an unlimited number of golf balls to hit, and most importantly a golf coach. Personal golf coaches range from $35 per hour up, so this will save you big money. (Conditions and fees vary at each school, so consult an admissions counselor)

46. An apple a day, well you've heard the rest. Actually "an apple a day keeps the doctor away," was a business slogan used to sell apples. But what if you were to buy a "Red Delicious Apple," a day at the current price of forty cent per apple?

> "Red Delicious Apple"
> lifelong cost =
> **$ 10,108.15***

These are just a few of the money saving ideas and fun things that I have experienced so far in life. Some of these ideas you may be already familiar with.

Want more money saving ideas?

There are many great resources online, just search "Money saving ideas" on Google.

In addition, check out the "Saving Money" section at www.theothersideofzero.com .

A few other common monthly expenses are,

> Netflix subscription
> lifelong cost =
> $ 24,917.37*

> A soda a day
> lifelong cost =
> $ 42,691.76*

> A $2.50 coffee a day
> lifelong cost =
> $ 63,157.22*

> One pack of cigarettes a day
> lifelong cost =
> $ 151,580.65*
> *not including medical expenses

How do I use the website to calculate what an expense will cost me over my lifetime?

There are two ways on the site to calculate what an expense will cost you over your lifespan,

1. Go to, http://www.theothersideofzero.com/incomeexpenseform.html .
   Enter your age, leave blank the number of monthly checks, leave blank the monthly income, leave blank amount in current savings, and **enter the amount of your expense for monthly expenses. Click submit.** The amount in the **total you have at retirement space** is the amount that expense would have cost you over your life.

Use the "Life Long Expenses" calculator link listed on the "Saving Money" page.

> *Grey box calculations are based off monthly total cost by not spending, average national expenses, and calculated for a person from the age of twenty-one to the estimated retirement age of sixty-five compounded annually at 1.926%.

Chapter 5
Rags to Rags

Carol's accounts begin to finally grow. As each debt she owes gets paid off and drops to the waste can, she has the feeling of finally becoming free. Her day to day worries are beginning to subside and the large cloud of debt that once prevented her from seeing has now turned into a light mist. Carol as a treat for herself for paying off debt starts to spend a little more than normal on clothes and jewelry. She gets her car cleaned one extra time per month and the people around her are starting to notice changes in her. She is carrying her head a little higher and walking a little straighter.

People ask Carol what she has been doing, and Carol responds with great excitement, "I almost paid off all my debts and my accounts just broke five thousand."

You would think Carol's friends and coworkers would be proud of her. You would think they would show support and tell her how good of a job she has been doing and tell her that getting out of debt is really hard and they are amazed at the visible changes in her life. This is the response Carol gets,

1. Questions about how she's doing it?
2. Questions about her helping them to do it.
3. Questions about borrowing money from Carol to help them pay a bill that is coming due.

Carol gets put into a position where she thinks her friend wants real advice, and then the situation turns into wanting to borrow money. What should Carol do? Carol knows that though she on the surface appears to have enough money to loan her friend, she would be only inhibiting her friend from learning the hard way. Carol tells her friend she can't loan her the money but will help her map out a plan to change her financial life. Carol's friend doesn't like Carol's offer because it doesn't help her immediately pay the upcoming bill that's due, and then begins to criticize Carol for not helping her. The criticism starts light like, "Must be nice!" and "I wish I could do that!" Then after a while her once thought of friend starts telling other acquaintances Carol's business and personal life. The people around Carol start to feel that she is showing off and start giving Carol the cold shoulder. Carol loses the relationships with the people that she once thought were friends, and doesn't understand why. What should Carol have done?

Carol should have not told her friends and coworkers about her life changing to the positive. Her friends and coworkers are going to notice the changes and ask about them, but Carol should only share that she is changing her life and that she learned about it from this book. Carol should not have shared being close to "debt free" or what the balances in her bank account are.

The people around you in life, if they are true friends are not going to criticize you. They are going to show support and pat you on your back. In the book, "The Millionaire Next Door: The Surprising Secrets of America's Wealthy," written by Thomas Stanley and William Danko, they discuss the typical millionaire and how the typical millionaire doesn't flaunt what they have. The millionaire next door is typically a normal person that doesn't drive fancy cars or wear designer suits. What I have experienced in life is dress the part of your profession. People in life treat you the way they perceive you. Wear an expensive suit or dress and drive an expensive car and people want things from you. Dress like a painter, and get treated like a painter. No one asks you for investment advice or money to pay a bill, because they don't think you have it. So the point is even though your bank accounts now have large balances in them, be careful of your outer image, and leery of who your true friends are. Dress your profession while at work and nothing more when you're not.

Chapter 6
Ramblings about All Things Financial

This chapter is a collective group of experiences that you should take into consideration. I would recommend getting bookmarks and marking the various sections that you find more intriguing and want to do more research into. Each section is separated by underlined bolded heading.

Medical Insurance

Not having medical insurance is one of the quickest ways to get into huge amounts of debt. The monthly expense of health insurance is sometimes one of the hardest expenses to justify when you feel healthy and you have so many other expenses that seem more important. Try to trim all your other monthly expenses before you decide to cut back on this one. This expense can easily save you thousands if not hundreds of thousands of dollars in the event of an illness or injury. Talk to an insurance company to discuss the best plans that are available for you and your family. If you get insurance through your employer set up a meeting with your employer and talk about your current coverage. Though I don't recommend cutting your insurance all together, adjusting it for your minimum needs is completely ok.

Think about this...

Will your life end if you knock out all of your teeth?

No.

So having huge dental coverage is probably not a necessity. But having annual cleanings and checkups is more important than you might think.

Like your automobile you must maintain your body. Neglect your car and it will break down more often with much higher repair costs. Preventative measures will save you money in the long run.

Ways to save when purchasing insurance?

Shop around. Different companies have different rates. Some employers have different plans based off need. Some schools require their students to pay health fees. Inquire about the health fees and what exactly is covered. Sometimes it's cheaper to be a part time student and pay health fees than it is to be on a non-student standard package plan that you might find online. Consult with an insurance specialist to discuss your insurance needs.

Don't smoke. Smoking increases your chance for many diseases and insurance companies charge more if you are a smoker.

Don't lie about your life. If you smoke or drink often, tell the insurance company you do. Your lying about your life can be an easy way for the insurer to deny your claim in the event of an illness or injury.

Call the insurance company every three to six months and ask for a better rate.

Ways to increase your per day income

The number one easiest way to increase your income now without decreasing your expenses is get a second job. A second job will provide you with enough money to cover some of your monthly expenses. A second job does not have to be fantastic. It just has to provide you with more income.

Start a home based business. A home based business provides you with not only additional income but also a tax write off (consult a tax attorney). There are numerous home based businesses that can provide you with decent extra income if you just do a little bit of work. A great place to get you started is http://www.entrepreneur.com/ . The site and monthly magazine covers various topics including types of home based businesses.

Investing in companies that pay dividends on a consistent, reliable basis is a fantastic way to increase you monthly income. Dividends are checks companies send you for being part owner. This is one of the easiest ways to increase your return on your money. Do research on high paying dividend stocks. A small investment can really turn into a lifelong stream of checks. This is one of my favorite additional income streams. If you don't know much about stocks and dividends consult a financial advisor and be sure to check out the bonus chapter at the end of this book entitled, "The Ramblings of an Average Joe Stock Trader."

Start a part time job in Real Estate. This is a fun profession in which you get to meet and work with a lot of different personalities and characters. Real Estate can provide you with a reliable income if you are willing to work hard and put forth the effort. Be honest, honest and honest and you will succeed. This profession does require state licensing and continuing education so be sure to check on your states requirements. Schedule a meeting with a local real estate broker to discuss your options and have any questions you may have answered.

Turn your hobby into a second profession. For example: If you love to make scrapbooks, why not start making scrapbooks for other people and making a dime off doing what you love.

Relocation

If you needed glasses but could not afford them would you sit in the back of the class or in the front?

If you can't afford life where you are currently pack up your things and move!

Just like in real estate location, location, location means everything. If you can't make it where you are at MOVE! It's as simple as that said out loud but is it that simple in real life? A move can be a difficult task that requires a lot of time and planning. Moving alone is much easier than moving a whole family, but it can be done. Sit down with your family and make a list of all the things you would like in an area. Be sure to address cultural activities, schools, temperature and climate, proximity to large cities and most importantly employment opportunities. Your surroundings could be the one thing that is holding you back in life. If your rent is astronomical or your fuel expense to commute is ridiculously high moving is always an option.

Don't be afraid to "Empty the pot!"

Debt is overwhelming. The phone doesn't stop ringing from debt collectors wanting your every penny. Notices in the mail seem to be non-stop. You would think if they saved the money from sending you all the bills they would surely pay off what you owe with what they save. Don't get hung up. Sometimes in life you have to except your losses and move on. If after working this system you come to the realization that the time and stress that you have impacting your life outweighs the living it is time to consult a professional bankruptcy attorney. Most people feel the word "bankruptcy" is life ending, but the reality is that millions of people do it and huge billion dollar companies do it. Society has imbedded this idea into our minds that "bankruptcy" is the end to you and your family. This is wrong. Your life does go on after bankruptcy. Though I do not recommend it as your first choice to being financially free it is an option and should not be taken off the table. Do more research on bankruptcy and consult a bankruptcy attorney if you feel this would be the right decision. I filed bankruptcy once early in my life. I ran into a situation where the amount I owed greatly exceeded the amount I made and was going to make for quite a while. I did research on the topic and consulted an attorney. We reviewed my options and decided that bankruptcy was the right decision. Sometimes in life, "if the soup is bad you have to empty the pot." You don't keep cooking or eating from a bad pot of soup, so why would you kill yourself struggling to keep your head above water for a few nickels and dimes. Life is worth more than that.

One thing you should know before we move on from this topic. If you don't fix your spending issues and your poor life decisions when it comes to money, bankruptcy will not help you. Bankruptcy could be like a new beginning, but if you didn't learn how to not be bankrupt you will in time just be in the same negative situation that you were in. If you decide to consult a bankruptcy attorney be sure to ask them if they are aware of any financial education courses that are provided in your area or online. This brings me to mention one of the top financial systems structured in a user friendly way out there. I will mention it because it is a complete detailed structured system that is, as you will find, the core of all not being in debt. Simply put he wrote down the basics and claimed fame to most debt topics, and then packaged it up to share with all willing to take the time to participate. You will find him on local radio stations and his books on the top selling book shelves. Over the years his packages seem to have become more and more of a commercial for addition products you can buy, or certain people you can use, but overall the information is good. The person I am speaking of is the New York Times bestselling author and host of the radio show "Dave Ramsey Show," Dave Ramsey. I would defiantly recommend checking out his information, you can find it at most public libraries and online. The statement I believe he is most known for and I have to agree it is an amazing statement is, "Live like no one else now so later you can live like no one else!"

The other big thing Dave Ramsey has been able to claim is the "Debt Snowball." It is the simple system of listing all your debts from smallest to largest and then paying them off in that order. Start at the smallest, pay it off, and then continue up the line using the "extra" money you have for the one you just paid off on the next one, until you are completely out of debt. Your probably wondering by now why am I mentioning Dave Ramsey in my book about debt? My response is there is no way to have a book about debt without mentioning him. If I don't any ideas that I have and suggest that are similar people will just classify me as a copycat and a plagiarist.

The second person I am going to mention is Suze Orman. Suze Orman is a financial planner and a television personality on, "The Suze Orman Show." Her information is wonderful to follow and give straight up advice about money and money management. The only issue I have with her show is she does a segment called, "Can I afford this?" She listens to callers stories and then determines if that person "can" or should buy or spend money on something. Time and time again I hear her say, "You can afford it!" to people that have debt. Guess what? If you owe anyone any amount of money for any reason then...

YOU CAN'T AFFORD IT,

YOU SHOULDN'T BE BUYING IT,

and

YOU DON'T HAVE THE MONEY!

The money you think you have belongs to someone else and that is where you should be putting it. There is one thing you should be buying if, "You can afford it," and that's a stamp so you can mail in a check to pay off the other people you owe money too.

Bank Draft and Automatic Payments

Be conscious of your money. Growing up, my mom always told me that you never go into a women's purse. A women's purse is her personal space. That is so ingrained in my head that to this day my wife gets a little upset with me when she asks me to get her phone out of her purse and I bring her the whole purse.

So I say to you, "Why are you letting complete strangers rummage through your purse or wallet?"

NEVER allow a company or business to draft payments from your accounts. Never give anyone access to withdraw for any reason. There are no justifiable reasons to allow this. Banks and lending institutions sometimes offer you special rates and perks for letting them do this, just say no thank you. If you can't spend two minutes transferring the money to them then you got greater time management issues that you should be dealing with.

Have you heard, "Going paperless saves the planet?" I am sure you have seen this with companies especially your bank. They encourage you to go paperless so you can help save the planet. The reality is the company is saying, "Save us time and money by not having to print and mail you statements so we can mail out more unsolicited junk credit card offers to people that don't know better." Hey I am for saving the planet but I am not for a company that is going to manipulate it customers into thinking they are doing something bad so the big company can save a dollar.

This now brings us to, when you donate a dollar for a worthy cause going through a grocery or department store checkout line, what you are actually doing is giving that company a dollar to donate, on <u>their</u> behalf, so they can look good in the public eyes and have a tax write off without having to actually spend any of their own money.

I am not saying don't donate when you can finally afford to donate. What I am saying is do research into what you are donating into. The dollar you give one place could be used more wisely by another organization that is more passionate about their cause; not passionate about getting more money.

<u>Simplify everything</u>

Haven't you ever felt bogged down or overwhelmed when working on a project? Make your life easier by getting rid of all the junk you have throughout your house or apartment. Have a garage sale and let it all go. Clean out your car including your trunk. You will be amazed at the feeling of freedom once you have emptied out all the unnecessary stuff in your life. You will find that freeing up space in your life also frees up space in your mind allowing you to work more efficiently. Clutter in one area of your life creates havoc in all areas of your life.

Why is paying off your house not a priority?

Paying off your house does have an incredible feeling but statistically for the majority of people it is not going to happen. It's not because it can't be done or that it's really hard because it's not. It does take time but the time it takes depends on how much you make and how much house you buy. Statistically people sell their homes every seven years. If every seven years people are relocating either for a job or just to move why bother killing yourself trying to pay it off. The same goes for fifteen year mortgages. I will get a lot of flak for this one but, why try to pay your house off in fifteen years. Yes it is nice to have a house paid for and yes you do save a ton of money by paying it off but…

What are you giving up in life while breaking your back trying to pay off your house?

- Time with your family,
- Time enjoying your hobbies,
- Time watching sunrises,
- Time watching time go by!

There are an unlimited number of things you could be doing but the number one for me is,

Living life! Living life entails all the above and so much more.

So you have two options when it comes to wanting to pay your house off,

1. Buy a really cheap house that is way below what you actually can afford, or

2. Come to the realization that a house payment is what you are always going to have and try to make the monthly payment as small as possible so you have money to enjoy LIFE.

Ok there is actually three, but most people won't put forth the effort to put this one into effect,

3. Buy a second house. Rent this second house out for enough to cover its expenses and at least part of your primary houses mortgage payment. This is one of the best ways to pay off your house, build equity, and build wealth. There are several great books on the market about this topic.

<u>Pennies</u>

If you are the type of person to walk by a penny and not spend the effort to pick it up, then what makes you think you will ever make the effort to have more than what you have right now?

Career Dreams

Imagine you want to open a scrapbook store. You need $15,000 to rent the location and buy all the necessary merchandise. Would you go out for dinner each night at an expensive restaurant, or would you stay at home and make a cheap meal?

If you needed a specific amount of money for doing your career dreams, why are you wasting the money on miscellaneous expenses that are not getting you closer to the dream? Until you turn your dream into a goal and make an effort to fulfill the goal, you are dreaming. A goal is a dream that is being put into action.

Upside Down

So you bought a car or a house and now it's worth less than what you still owe. What are your options?

1. Continue to pay the loans as per your agreement at the time of the signing of the contract.
2. Stop paying the loans, destroy your credit.
3. Sell the car or house for what it's worth and take out a loan for the remaining balance. Some financial institutions will help you set up a loan to cover the remaining difference. But what if your credit is now ruined because you haven't been able to make the payments, and the bank won't give you a loan to cover the difference?

If you have exhausted all avenues to recover and you are still spinning your wheels it is time to stop, breath, and consult a financial planner to determine what course of action is best for your financial situation. Every person's situation in life is different. You can only do so much, and unless you have an extensive background in business and finance you need to consult a licensed professional.

Saving your way to a raise

You have a job that pays you $15 per hour. You need more money so you ask your boss for a raise. The boss says. "Do to the economy we will not be able to provide you with the raise you desire." What now?

Start aggressively increasing the amount you're saving and the interest you receive will act like a raise. Most people are excited if they receive a $.25 raise. That is equivalent to $10 per week if you work a forty hour work week.

How much money do you have to have in an account to be equal to $10 per week?

$.25 per hour = $2.00 per day

$2.00 per day x 260 work days per year = $520 per year

$520 per year / 4% (decent interest rate) = $13,000

You need only $13,000 getting a 4 percent interest rate to get a $.25 per hour raise.

So, in a roundabout way, for less than the cost of an average new car you could get a raise of $.25 in hourly pay by just having $13,000.

The average car loan lasts approximately five years. So instead of buying a car save the money and get a raise every five years.

(See also the section entitled, "Critical Mass, The Ultimate of All Numbers")

My Change of View

I used to think getting ahead in life was all about two things, how much money you have and who you know. I have since realized I was wrong. One of the above two statements is wrong. Do you know which one it is?

Getting ahead in life is not determined by how much money you have. Getting ahead in life is all about what you know! Know enough about a subject, (and I cannot stress the word enough) and people will pay you any amount you ask for that information.

The second statement above still holds true. If you don't know anyone to share the information with or who wants it, the information becomes worthless.

Saving for Retirement

A percentage of every dollar you earn is supposed to go towards your retirement when you reach the age of 66. You get paid (so called) bonuses for delaying your retirement to the age of 70. If you wait till 70 to retire your maximum pay will be $3,119.00 per month.

Read more at

http://www.nasi.org/learn/socialsecurity/retirement-ge?gclid=CJas4brfjrECFWVOTAodHAURNw

That's only $779.75 a week. And guess what? Since the total annual amount is above the $25,000 (for singles) and $32,000 (for married) you get to pay federal taxes on the income. So now you get to pay taxes on money that was collect by taxes for your retirement. You are paying taxes on your taxes.

Read more at,

http://ssa-custhelp.ssa.gov/app/answers/detail/a_id/493/~/paying-income-tax-on-social-security-benefits

Now let's talk retirement insurance!

Insurance companies calculate the odds of having to pay out on policies. They do research to determine risk and try to reduce the possibility of payout. (Just like casinos) The higher the risk the higher the premium. The

US census estimates the average person will live to 78.9 by 2015 and to 79.5 years of age by the year 2020.

http://www.census.gov/compendia/statab/2012/tables/12s0104.pdf

Social security is an insurance policy that we pay into over our lives. The odds of us reaching the age expectancy keeps increasing hence the government needs to keep increasing the age of retirement.

Unrealistic Numbers (big numbers)

Many people have a hard time comprehending really big numbers like one hundred thousand, or one million. Many people have a hard time comprehending just two to three thousand dollars. For you to understand and comprehend numbers better you must get comfortable with larger numbers. You must find a way for you to be able to relate to the number. For example a car, an average Honda Civic, depending on features and area of the country, is approximately $19,876.00. But since you make monthly payments of only $353.36 per month, you can only relate to the car costing $353.36 per month. You have no fixed emotion to the total price; your emotion is only tied to the amount per month price. Why do you think an auto dealer says to you when you ask about price, "How much do you want your car payments to be?" It is easier for our brains to relate to numbers that we are more familiar with.

Why do you need to be comfortable with larger numbers?

In the above example you don't owe $353.36 per month. You owe the total balance of $19,867.00. Breaking it up into smaller amounts is just a way to trick your mind and justify you being able to afford it. In the moment of purchase you don't realize that over the life of the loan you are paying $25,441.92 (amount calculated at 6% for 6 years). That's $5,565.92 more than the cost of the car. Or put a different way that is an extra $77 per month. Doesn't seem like much does it? But the reality is, it is!

Getting used to bigger numbers and the appreciation of the amount of hours put into creating those bigger numbers, is a key in controlling spending. If you at the moment of purchasing a red sweater take into account the number of hours it takes you to work to come up with the money to purchase the sweater you may have a second thought saying don't buy, don't buy. Would you dig ditches in the hot sun for ten hours straight for a new pair shoes? How many hours does it take you to work for the amount you paid for your car?

Taking Vacation

Poor people can't afford to go on a vacation. What are you taking a vacation from, being poor? Cash in your vacation days and use that money to pay your bills. No stress, from being debt free, is like making everyday a vacation.

Remember there are only two ways to change your financial future,

1. Increase your income, or
2. Decrease your debt.

Ideally you want to do both. Make the short term sacrifice and do both to the maximum and wealth is inevitable.

There are two types of interest

We mentioned the two types of interest earlier in this book but we want to stress this topic so we are covering it again here.

There are two main types of interest. Simply put what you pay someone else, and what others pay you.

The first one, what you pay someone else, is the bad evil witch interest that you want as little to do with as possible. We don't want to have to pay someone else for anything. There are certain circumstances where this is unavoidable. If you buy a house, most people don't have all the cash to pay for the entire balance so they take out a loan for the house. They pay interest. This interest is not good but a necessary interest if you want to have a home and build equity without paying someone rent until you have enough to purchase the house in cash.

The book, "Rich Dad Poor Dad" written by Robert Kiyosaki does a good job of explaining the various types of assets and liabilities including interest on money.

The second type of interest, what others pay us, is the good witch interest. This interest is what others pay us for loaning our money to others. Say you loan Carol five dollars for one week. After a week she gives you back six dollars. The one dollar you made off your investment of five dollars is interest. For our purposes we are going to see interest as any amount of money returned for any amount of money put in

(Want greater details see also ROI or return on investment capital at http://en.wikipedia.org/wiki/Rate_of_return)

A simple solution to identity theft

Identity theft is a growing problem. Each day a new scam involving identity theft makes the evening news. A simple and effective way to halt identity theft (at least short term) is to issue all persons with a social security number a second number similar to a CSC number. If you look on the back of your debit or credit card you will see some additional numbers. Those numbers are called CSC or card security code. For more information pertaining to the CSC check out http://en.wikipedia.org/wiki/Card_security_code .

Buying a new car versus a used car

The decision of buying a new car or a used car is quite a challenge. Do you want the new car smell, and the security in knowing that you're not going to be stranded somewhere do to a used car breakdown? Many people believe that buying a new car is a poor decision. The idea that a new car drops in value the moment you drive it off the lot is relatively true, but…

A new car gets lower insurance rates because of its added safety features such as air bags and antilock brakes that typically weren't available on older models. A new car has less of a chance of breaking down as long as it's maintained properly. A new car is safer to drive in the event you are in an automobile accident. Newer cars normally will be more fuel efficient than used cars.

Do you want to drive around with your children in a 1981 car with very few safety features? Do you want an automobile payment? Some states have property taxes on automobiles so you may have to pay higher taxes, do you want that?

A used car is typically cheaper than a new model. The fuel expense is typically higher because it gets a fewer miles per gallon. The maintenance on older models is cheaper. The insurance appears to be less on older cars but that is only because it is an older car and the insurance company doesn't have to pay out as much in the event of an accident. An older requires shorter time between maintenance intervals depending upon make.

When buying new or used the sensible decision typically leans towards used, and I would agree if paying cash. If you are buying a new car it typically will go down in value when you drive it off the lot, meaning you immediately lose money. The amount lost depends on the make and model. If you buy a new car on credit you typically get a lower interest rate than you would if you buy a used car on credit. If you run the numbers the used cars interest rate typically becomes an equal amount as the depreciation of the new cars value drops when driving off the lot. This varies greatly on lender, make, model, and credit score. Many people do not take this difference in interest rate into consideration when purchasing an automobile. Am I saying buy a new car?

No what I am saying is do your research, not only on the car, but the interest rate on new versus used. If you can buy a used car for the same interest rate as a new then you have to take into account insurance rates, maintenance costs, fuel expenses, etc.

Life is about balance and consistency. Too far in one direction and you will tip the scales.

You will be giving something up if you're going to change your financial life. Most people's debt was created on impulse purchases that they created as they were living life. Now they have to play catch-up and pay for it.

Making donations

It is one of the greatest opportunities in the world to be able to share wealth with others. Many of the world's most famous and wealthiest people spend their lives making money only to later share that wealth with others. In no way do I discourage helping others but,

Would you ask a poor, starving person for their last can of soup so you then can give it to someone else whom may or may not need it?

Would you give the money to someone who is asking if you knew they were going to make a small profit off of the transaction of helping someone else?

Guess what? If you have debt you are not in a position to assist anyone financially. You should be saving those donations to get yourself out of debt so you can do some real good with the interest that you're earning off your money. Ponder this... Can you help someone who wants money more if you give them your last dollar, or can you help them more by using that dollar to make another dollar and then giving it to them?

So many charities and organizations ask us for monetary donations but don't ask us for physical assistance. Next time someone asks for your help by you donating money, ask them how you can help without donating money.

To reiterate: If you are negative zero you are poor. You need to be helping yourself first and making a list of who you will help when you get to the plus side of zero.

Most of the time they say your money will help them more than your services. Do research on who you choose to donate money to.

Directly helping another person by education, sharing your food, or even lending an ear are ways you can help. Giving does not always have to be about money.

Remember now is the time you should be catching up and getting out of debt.

Yes I know what you're thinking, I hear it all the time and I thought the same thing in the beginning,

"I want to have a life."
"I don't want to sit at home and do nothing."

Author and radio personality, Dave Ramsey said it best,

"Live like no one else now,
so later you can live like no one else!"

Chapter 7
Doing It Together "Coupling Love and Finances"

Communication is the number one priority when it comes to relationships. Communication about money is one of the most difficult topics you will probably experience. Most problems in a relationship, especially those that fail, can be traced to money. We don't have enough money, your spending too much, why do you leave the lights are all questions and arguments that are going to happen if you don't share what you're working for.

You must communicate with your partner. You must discuss where you are at and where you plan on going. You must work together to achieve your goals.

But before you talk you must realize that people have different goals. What you want and what they want could be completely different. You don't ask someone to be a doctor that doesn't want to be a doctor. You can share with them about your life plans but you can't make them change their plans to fit yours.

EXAMPLE- Jane wants a master's degree in biology. Jane has been working her whole life to achieve this. When you met Jane you knew her level of drive and passion towards getting that degree. You want to save money and that is your passion. Jane takes out student loans to pay for school and doesn't work because she doesn't have the time and energy for both. What should you do?

Share with Jane what you are working towards. Support Jane in continuing her dreams. Adapt to the situation to absorb the additional debt. That's part of being in a relationship.

"Saving money is a lot like having sex; it is always more fun when you're not alone!"

The three most important things to know when dealing with love and money is,

1. <u>Communication is empirical</u>- Share with your partner what you're trying to achieve and express to them the life you want to be living. A team effort is a whole lot easier when you are doing it together and the speed at which you can get out of debt and build your accounts is super-fast.

2. <u>Realization is key</u>- Realizing that if your partner doesn't want to participate in your "getting out of debt lifestyle" they don't have to. You just have to work harder at making up the difference. Don't get upset just work harder. Their goals don't have to be your goals. Simply ask your partner to give up charging and try to save a little. Express to them that any amount of saving helps. By asking you will get a much better response than telling.

3. <u>Love is everything</u>- Discussions elevating to arguments, then escalating to fights are pointless. Your relationship is more important than money. Arguments over money is what a good marriage counselor is for. If you find that you and your partner are spending more time arguing about money than making money, it is time for you to find help and guidance from a specialist that has dealt with similar situations. Only fools don't ask for help.

Chapter 8
No "U" Turns

As your debt shrinks and your accounts begin to grow you will get to certain points where you feel you can afford things that you should not be buying. Most people when they reach certain amounts want to buy, buy, buy. And if you give in to these urges I can guarantee you one thing, you will be waiving your money bye, bye, bye. And everything you have worked so hard to achieve would have been a waste of time…or was it. Look I know you're going to give in and buy something or spend on something you know you shouldn't have. We all do it. The thing you must realize is that you just need to take a small step back and recover your losses. Don't be disappointed or get too upset, just realize you made a mistake and move forward.

Do not block the intersection- Talking to other people and surrounding yourself with likeminded people.

Those around you are going to judge you and criticize your cutting back decisions. Don't let those around you influence your life. This is the way it works, 1. You start cutting back, 2. Those you know will start remarking on you being cheap, or some other negative comment, 3. Your debts start going down, 4. Your accounts start to get fat, 5. Those same people that were critical before start asking you if you can help them fix their situation. The same cycle will repeat itself every time you have a small set back so don't let it bother you. Realize this is the way it is and move forward. Find similar minded people and form a small group. Get together once a week and share ideas about saving and investing. What works for you could be what the other person was trying to figure out and what works for them could be what you were looking for. With modern technology like Facebook, and Twitter it should be real easy to find likeminded people. Post on your page the phrase, "I am working on getting to the other side of zero." In time you will be amazed at how many other people are too.

Be prepared for the money roadblocks!

There are going to be certain amounts of money that you can't seem to break through. My most difficult ones were at $3000, $8000, $11000, $18000 and $47000. I like to call these numbers roadblocks because each time I approached going up and through them I would have some surprise expense that would knock me back down (typically three surprise expenses).

I can't predict what amounts will be your roadblocks but I can say to you this, "You will know it when you get to them."

"Is there a way around the roadblock?"

No, there is no way around the roadblock. Just know they are coming and try to recognize them as quickly as possible. As soon as you recognize it tighten your belt and hold on for the short financial ride. Push, push, push till you get to the other side and financially stabilize. Just like going into the roadblock you will know when you get to the other side. I typically experience a quick pop in the balance as soon as I push through, and stabilize.

Get the money off you. Break it up. Make it hard to get to. I know this seems like the opposite of what I told you earlier when you were trying to get out of debt, but mentally now that you actually have money splitting it up is the better choice. Now you have to trick your brain into thinking you have less. I like no less than three accounts. One primary checking, one secondary checking, and one online brokerage. The first checking account is where all deposits go. I like to have this as my first line of defense. I put money in, expenses come out. Direct deposit if I am forced to have it goes into this account. If you are forced to have money drafted from your account this is the account it would be, though I highly recommend not allowing access to anyone other than your spouse or caregiver. The second checking account is where I move the money from the first account once it reaches a certain level. I like the even number of four thousand. When the first account gets to four thousand I move most of the balance to the second account. The second account is the emergency backup for the first account. In the event a surprise expense (injury, weather damage, accident, etc.) occurs I quickly move funds over to the first account. Once the second account hits four thousand I then move most of the money into the online brokerage account. I use Scottrade as my online broker. They now offer banking services but I just like the standard account. This account allows me the opportunity to move money into and out of stocks, and mutual funds with a couple keyboard strokes. It also pays a small amount of interest on my money not tied up in securities. The brokerage account is free to open and they charge no inactivity fees. Check them out at www.scottrade.com . I have not had enough time to fully check out their online banking so I can't say I am for it or against it. Do your research and always talk to a financial specialist prior to making any investment or financial decisions.

If you decide to open an account be sure to check out the bonus excerpt later in this book entitled, "The Ramblings of an Average Joe Stock Trader, 2nd Edition." It leans more towards short term trading but is a good place to start.

Chapter 9
Zero and Beyond

Far beyond the dollar - Going beyond the standard bank interest rate.

So you are wondering, "I am now out of debt, and can work at putting chunks of money away, how do I get the maximum return on my money?" "Where can I put my money to get the highest ROI (return on investment)?" and "What is critical mass?"

Following is a list of places you can maximize your return on your money. Each has its own risks and rewards, headaches and problems, and gains and losses, so I highly suggest you do research and discuss these various investments with your financial planner before jumping in head first. A great book to help get you started in understanding why some of these investments are so fantastic is, "The Little Book That Beats the Market," by

Joel Greenblatt. In this book he explains using simple easy to understand examples about how the market works and why different investments have different returns.

Places to put your money to work

1. The standard bank account
2. Money market account
3. Real Estate
4. Stocks (dividend paying, large-cap, etc.)
5. Mutual Funds
6. Municipal Bonds
7. Commodities
8. Futures
9. **Education**- Sometimes the greatest return can be made off investing in yourself. Take some classes at a local community college or finish off that degree you have always wanted. Spending a little money now on educating yourself can pay off huge in the long run.
10. Cash- "Why would cash be on this list?" 10% of your total investment should always be in cash. If the market takes a dip or the real estate market goes south, opportunities always present themselves. If you have all your free capital tied up in investments you will miss out on these fantastic money making opportunities. Some of the easiest money I have ever made has been on really big stock market down days.

The point in this simple list is to get your mind rolling about ideas that stimulate other ideas. Diversifying your money among different types of investments is a good way to prevent losses in the event of unpredicted surprises. Know your risk before making any investment and always consult a specialist in the field you are thinking about investing.

You might think to yourself, "If I could just come up with the next big idea then…" My response to this is, **"Repeat what successful people have already done to the point you are extremely successful. Then in your free time revolutionize the system."**

One more note,

Diversification is a word used often to convince you to spread your money so thin amongst a bunch of investments, that you will be lucky if you get a great return on anything. Diversification is what people that have money do. The key word in the previous sentence was HAVE. Try to buy a stock or a house with just a few hundred dollars and you will quickly see you can't get much of anything that is going to return decent money. There is a minimum amount of money you need before diversification is even an option. Don't be fooled when you hear you should be diversified. Pay attention and start asking questions. I have found (for me) the minimum amount of money that can begin to be spread out amongst different investments (diversified) is roughly $10,000.

Critical mass, the ultimate of all numbers

We all want to be wealthy. We all want so much money that we never really have to think about money again.

What do you think that amount of money would be for you?

So that brings us to my favorite number, critical mass.

What is Critical Mass and how do you calculate it?

Critical mass is defined by Wikipedia as,

(Pay special attention to the wording of the second definition)

> Noun
>
> critical mass (plural critical masses)
>
> 1. (physics) the amount of fissile material that is needed to support a self-sustaining nuclear chain reaction
>
> 2. A quantity or amount required to trigger a phenomenon.
>
> http://en.wiktionary.org/wiki/critical_mass

Critical mass for the financial world is

The minimum amount of money required that yields enough interest or return off itself to sustain your current life style without working. Meaning the total money you have, makes enough interest that you can live your life "presently" without working another day.

I would say that's a "phenomenon" wouldn't you?

You don't need 100 million dollars.

You don't need 10 million dollars.

You don't even need 1 million dollars.

The amount of critical mass you need is only enough to cover the expenses of your daily life.

So let's say you spend fifty-six dollars a day.

How much do you need to have in the bank, in a standard savings account, to give you enough interest to be equal to fifty-six dollars per day?

For this example we are using 1% interest paid monthly with compounding interest. This is a crude example of this calculation but you will understand the point.

$30,000 (cash) x 0.01 (monthly interest rate at bank in standard savings)/ 12 (months in year) = approximately $30 month or $1 a day.

$56 (spend per day needed) x $30,000(cash) = $1,680,000 (approximate amount needed in cash or CM)

Get a higher interest rate or return on your investment (ROI) and you need less critical mass. The supposed average rate of return for investing in the stock market over the last eighty or so years has been 12%. Get 12% (consistently) and you can go work on Wall Street. I like to use 4% for this calculation. It's not too high and unrealistic but it's not so low that it's ridiculous. When you have more money you get higher rates of return. You will know when you reach what's considered above normal when the teller at the bank keeps asking you to open up higher interest paying accounts that are not listed on the fancy brochures or signs in the lobby.

Same equation ran with 4% interest,

$30,000 (cash) x 0.04 (monthly interest rate)/ 12 (months in year) = approximately $100 month or $3.29 a day.

$56 (spend per day)/3.29(interest per day) = 17.02

17.02 x $30,000 = $510,630 (approximate amount needed in cash or your critical mass)

So you need approximately $510,000 in a bank account getting 4% or 0.04 to earn enough interest to pay your $56 per day expenses.

Working a normal job you must make no less than approximately $25,000 per year to cover the $56 per day expenses. And that is breaking even.

The average high school graduate in the United States makes on average $37,683.50 per year.

http://www.census.gov/compendia/statab/2012/tables/12s0703.pdf

How much money does a person have to have in critical mass to sustain what an average high school graduate will make per year?

Approximately $950,000.00

Could you imagine making in interest on your money what a high school graduate makes per year working?

One million dollars invested in an account paying 4% compounded monthly returns approximately $4,000 per month.

> Except for the previous examples, I typically like to use one percent for most of my calculations. I consider anything above the one percent a bonus.

To find some of the best savings and money market rates in your area check out,

https://www.google.com/advisor/ussavings

Life is like playing video games. Most video games have multiple settings of difficulty, easy, normal and hard. Always play on the hardest setting and everything else becomes easy.

Next Up, Bonus Materials

This book includes two bonus excerpts of "The Ramblings of an Average Joe Stock Trader, 2nd Edition," and "Real Estate 101 Profit Max!!!" I have included these two excerpts because these are the things I enjoy and that I have found have given me the greatest return on money. When I was around twenty years old, I started asking the wealthy people I met what their profession was. They all responded with either real estate or stock investing. At the time real estate was the easiest for me to understand and get into, so I first chose that. As the economy changed and my bank accounts grew I started exploring the stock market and trading stocks. Of the two different paths I find the stock market the most exciting with the greatest potential for unlimited gains (and losses). I put these two excerpts in this book so you could explore avenues that you may find interesting once you're on the other side of zero.

Do you remember this in chapter one?

"Stop, take this book and go to your car. Slightly adjust your seat so the back sits..."

The reason why I had you change your seat position was to demonstrate to you how a simple small change can make your life a little uncomfortable in the beginning, but in time the uncomfortable becomes the new normal.

By now you should be on the road to your new normal. The uncomfortable changes you have made to your financial life should now be revealing themselves in a new form. A form of stress free living that not only gives you peace of mind but a little spending money on the side.

Simple changes can equal BIG results.

Keep trying,

stay focused on the numbers,

and don't forget your childlike enthusiasm.

From the author,

Thank you for reading, "The Other Side of Zero." We hope you enjoyed the book and encourage you to share it with others. The following two chapters are bonus chapters to give you a small sampling of two different income paths that I recommend you explore. These two excerpts are about by favorite two topics, stocks and real estate. The topics covered in each book are my sources of additional income streams and how I get higher rates of return than what is in a standard savings account.

The first excerpt is the first chapter from the book, "The Ramblings of an Average Joe Stock Trader, 2nd Edition." This book is a collection of all of the information I learned through trial and error when I first started trading the United States stock market.

The second excerpt is the first section of the book, "Real Estate 101 Profit Max!!!" This book is about 101 ways to save money when investing in real estate. The tips and ideas included in this section are things that I have used throughout my years of investing in real estate that have made me, or saved me money. This small section alone will give you enough small advice that you should be able to save hundreds if not thousands on your first home purchase or real estate investment.

I recommend reading both bonus excerpts and exploring each different investment pathway.

Good luck in all your adventures, I hope they are very exciting and what you have always dreamed they would be.

Christopher L. Boyer

Bonus Excerpt of
"The Ramblings of an Average Joe Stock Trader"
All the information I wish I knew in the beginning!

CONTENTS

	Acknowledgments	i
1	TO START WITH	1
2	THE DISCLAIMERS	3
3	THE BASICS	14
4	BRIEF RAMBLINGS	25
5	CHOOSING A BROKERAGE	27
6	IT'S ALL ABOUT THE MONEY	29
7	THE POWER OF MULTIPLE SHARES	32
8	BUYING ON MARGIN, AND THE $25,000 RULE	34
9	THE MEAT OF THE BOOK "THE RAMBLINGS OF AN AVERAGE JOE STOCK TRADER"	40
10	OTHER RAMBLINGS OF WISDOM NOT NECESSARILY PERTAINING TO STOCKS	110
	RECOMMENDED READINGS, SITES, AND PROGRAMS	114

(Content page image from "The Ramblings of an Average Joe Stock Trader, 2nd edition")

FREE TRADES THAT WILL PAY FOR THIS BOOK

I told you that this book pays for itself in multiple ways, here's one. If you open an online brokerage account with www.scottrade.com, during the
"OPENING THE ACCOUNT"
stage enter the information below. You will get three free trades. If Scottrade charges $7 dollars for every trade, and you get three free then you just saved $21 dollars, more than the cost of this book!

Referred by: CHRISTOPHER LEE BOYER
ReferALL code: UQTD5579

Be sure to enter the code when asked during the online application process or at the local branch office when you open the account.

The average individual believes that investing in the stock market is just a gamble. They believe their hard earned dollars have the same odds of multiplying on a casino craps table, as they do in the market. The truth is the market is what you make it. Little do they realize what their 401K plan is, or that the value of their house in a roundabout way is closely tied to the stock market. Investing in the market is very similar to buying a house. Most individuals don't buy a house by just knowing its address. They investigate the area, check out the schools, have it inspected, have an appraisal done and walk through it a couple times, all before buying. You can blindly buy a house, or you can do all the research you can to make sure you are making a sound investment. Like your home the more research, time and effort you put forth, the greater your opportunity of increasing your overall risk/return ratio, hence more profits. Investing short-term and long-term in the market is the only endeavor I have found that provides you with the greatest opportunity of magnifying your current financial situation with unlimited possibilities in the shortest amount of time. Your financial future is only dependent upon your willingness to explore, learn, and experience the market.

Your adventure begins here!

THE DISCLAIMERS

Read slow. Every line in this book contains more than just a thought or concept. Every line, even though written simple, has great meaning with many hours of time tested experience behind it. If you do not comprehend the sentences, I truly encourage you to do research on each topic to the point you do fully understand. Don't move slow and you will lose money!

Go to "Staples Office Supply" and get some STICKIES. Mark the pages with the STICKIES, and label them. This will make it easy to flip to the individual topic sections. Add your own notes to these pages and sections. In this second edition I have tried to provide room for notes. Another good idea is to start a three ring notebook.

In a way this is the first chapter. You should understand this section to be able to understand the rest. This is not going to be a normal book. Many passionate readers that bought the first edition wanted more details, note sections, and input lines included in the book to help them fill in and learn as they go along. One of the main suggestions from the readers of the first edition of "The Ramblings of an Average Joe Stock Trader," was to make this book more like a workbook that they can go back too periodically to review and reflect on what they have learned. They wanted areas to jot notes and input ideas. In this edition we have tried to fill everyone's requests. And like the first edition all your input is welcome and we all thank you for helping shape this book. We welcome your ideas, stories and input. Tell us what works for you and what doesn't. We are all learning together.

Send suggestions, questions and comments to clboyer7@gmail.com. In the subject line you should type "book, 2nd edition." We will try to respond to every email in a timely and efficient manner, just be patient.

This book is a composite of all the knowledge I have learned trading the market whether it was a positive or negative experience. I once took my dogs out for 5 minutes just to come back to learn I was now down $800. That is when I learned to never leave a short term position unattended. So when you talk to traders make sure they tell you about their down days equally as much as their up days. Most active traders know that it is the down days that you will learn the most from and in the long run, profit the most from.

I have tried to include all my experiences, so that you can learn from my mistakes, and success. I starting out had no one to teach me the ropes, or to mentor me. No one was there to hold my hand or guide me as my accounts climbed then sank. For me it has been a lot of trial and error learning, reading books, asking questions, and just flat out doing. The best way to learn to trade is just start. Most people stand on the sidelines waiting for that moment that never comes. Your first step is, like Nike says "just do it." The sooner you get started the sooner you will have a better understanding and a clue.

Most of those around you will have their own interpretation of the market. Most of those around you will have a 401K plan and interpret the market as a long term investment, yet they don't know why. Analysts and brokers say historically you would have yielded a 10% to 12% return if you started investing about 80 years ago. What they don't tell you is, yes you would have got that return if you started out investing on an exact date and time so long ago, but if you would have started investing, let's say 2 years ago (2007), you would be down big if you were a long term investor. Time frame is an interpretation of the individual making the argument or graph. Time frame if not given is the interpretation of the listener.

You will quickly realize that those around you don't have much of a real idea about the market and trading. The most they have experienced is their local nightly news or a newspapers business section. Unless you are of the select and fortunate you will find few people to talk too, share ideas with, and trade with. As you advance in your quest for more knowledge about the market you will find fewer and fewer people to converse with. You will understand what I mean the first time you sit down with someone and find yourself trying to explain what a Bollinger band is or an inverted head and shoulders pattern. Most of your conversations will consist of you explaining how trading is different than gambling and the basic terms and phrases. Most of your conversations will be you bringing others up to speed.

In no way do I claim to know it all. I know I am still learning. Before I began trading I thought to myself if I could understand trading stocks as much as I understood making money in real estate I will be unbelievably successful. What I have learned since is, the more you think you know about the market the bigger the market is. To comprehend it all is not possible. You must only understand what you need too and nothing more. Repeat, repeat and repeat. Find a successful system and run it into the ground. I also realize that I must give thanks to everyone out there that has helped develop my neural pathways, whether directly or indirectly. Thank you!

At the end of this book I have listed a few of my favorite educational resources pertaining to the market and why I felt those individual items were so beneficial to my success.

This book is written in a straight to the point format with tips, stories and ideas written in a short direct manor. You may find some sections of this book choppy and not flowing. My point in writing this book was not to become a great author but to assist those like me out there find an answer. The point of this book is to help those out there learn just a little bit more about trading and investing. Many of the things in this book you will not find in chat rooms, books, blogs or videos. I am positive that there is at least one piece of information in this book that if you grasp will pay for this book many times over. I only wish someone would have told me the contents of this book when I was first starting to paper trade. This book would have saved me hundreds of hours and thousands of dollars.

You will find that sections of this book are written in a fashion that I only note topics that you should understand or learn. Example—Learn what a "wash sale" is.

In this 2nd edition we have inserted lines following for you to fill in, jot notes, or just write down ideas. The reason I only note the topic is so you can do your own research. I am not trying to duplicate other writer's books, lectures, and websites or just hand the answers to you. The best way to learn is by doing. To understand an idea you must comprehend the idea to its deepest level. I believe in the saying, "you can give a man a fish and he will eat for a day, or you can teach a man to fish and he will eat forever."

I use Scottrade as my online broker. www.scottrade.com. The $7 dollar online trades are decent, but compared to the other online brokers the amount of information that they give a beginner without additional fees, more than pays for itself. Don't get hung up on trying to find the cheapest trade commission. Look for a broker that provides you with the most useful information, for the least amount of money. Make sure they have no inactivity fees. The great thing about Scottrade is you can open up an account online in about 10 minutes, and you have immediate access to an abundance of tools and a great knowledge section. They have web videos on how to use their platforms and setting up. Though, they don't go into great detail about how to actively trade and what to look for in a chart patterns.

The other great thing about Scottrade is they pay interest on your account cash balance even if you are not active. It is just like a standard bank account that provides you with the ability to be able to move your money in and out of stocks, mutual funds, and options. The interest rate on the checking account is low but it beats the 0% you're getting on your national chain checking account.

Scottrade also insures your money for a lot more than your standard banks FDIC. If you decide to use Scottrade as your online broker you should inquire about how your money is protected and what amount it is insured for. They do not insure you for making bad investment decisions.

A downfall that Scottrade has is it has a way to virtual trade the market in real-time, but you can only do that with the Scottrade Elite platform which requires you to deposit $25,000. I know when I first started out I didn't have the $25,000 needed for the advanced platform, but in time I worked hard at coming up with it. So paper trade. We will discuss that later in this book.

The main differences in the Scottrade Elite platform and the standard platform is you have access to NASDAQ Level II, and Trade Ideas. We will discuss those later in this book. You do not need these two tools to trade, so don't worry about having less than $25,000 to start out with. Don't go out and borrow your grandmother's savings thinking you need it to start!

Times change, situations change, the market changes. Think of the market as a living organism. It wakes up and sleeps at different times. The news feeds the market, and the market can bleed. All of the information contained in this book are my findings at the time I found them. You should understand that the market changes from second to second and adjustment in style and thought is necessary to adapt and be profitable. In time the light bulb in your head will go off, and you will start to see the big picture.

Before you make any investment decisions you should always consult your financial advisor. They will have many ideas about the market and should have an abundance of literature on investing.

This book is only a situational, workbook style tip guide to share my experiences and learning's with you. You will quickly find that there is much more than just one way of doing, trading, and investing. Do what works best for you.
You should also know that this book is written based on

EAST coast time. So all references to time are based on east coast time. You should make adjustments to compensate for your time zone. If you're in San Diego the market lunch time moody blues does not happen between 11am and 1:15pm. It occurs between 8am and 10:15am. So don't forget to adjust for your time zone. An easy way to adjust is put a clock on the wall and set it to east coast time (New York Time).

I do not work for, and am in no way compensated or sponsored by Scottrade. I have no affiliation with Scottrade other than being a customer myself. They have not paid me to promote their company and they make no claims as to the validity of any statements or concepts included in this book pertaining to them. You should use, who you choose best fits your style of investing.

Finally some of the information contained in this book may be simple for you. But not everyone starts in the same place. I find that some of the easier tasks and simple things to understand are the most easily forgotten.

Things to learn and do:
Familiarize yourself with various online brokers
Consult a financial advisor
Consult a tax attorney
Some interesting and fun things to do!
As you start your journey down Wall Street, you may quickly realize there is an overwhelming amount of information to absorb. As your understanding and thoughts change about the market you may feel your senses become quickly overpowered. It's a lot of information. But the sooner you start the easier trading will be in time.

This is not a get rich quick kind of game. To be in the game for the long run it takes a lot of time, thought and energy. These are a few fun exercises that make the learning experience a little more enjoyable.

1) Get some multicolor highlighter pens. Highlight the sections in this book that you find most interesting or you realize that you just had one of those "aha" moments. Then in a different color, highlight those things you do not completely understand. As time passes and you continue your search for more knowledge come back and read this book again. Use another color highlighter. You will be amazed at the amount of information you have learned, understand, agree with, and disagree with. Pay special attention to the overlapping colors.

2) Find and watch a few stock movies.
"The Trillion Dollar Bet," PBS,
"The Warning," PBS,
"Boiler Room" is interesting
--And of course the infamous
"Wall Street and "Wall Street (2)
In six months watch these same movies again. Notice how the first time you watched them you followed the story but did not get the details. The second time you watch them you will be amazed at the number of words and phrases you first did not hear or pay attention to. Notice how your lack of familiarity with the topics discussed made your interpretation of the movie slightly different.

Learning and understanding the vocabulary words
is like surround sound for your mind!

3) Find some likeminded people that you can start this journey with. Understanding the market and what moves it is much easier if you have other minds to bounce ideas and concepts off of. If you wait too long to share with others you will find that your knowledge far exceeds theirs and you will spend most of your conversational time bringing them up to speed on terminology, phrases and basic ideas. Start a group or investment club. Stay away from the online message boards like Yahoo. Message boards can manipulate you into and out of trades based on nothing more than rumors and lies. Overtime these message boards can become a useful tool but not for an inexperienced trader.

4) Create a notebook. When I state "Do more
research," or "Learn more," actually do the homework and input those sections and notes into your notebook. At the end of this book if you spent the time to create a notebook on all the topics suggested you will have a source of information that you will use for years to come.

Want to read more?

Check out the book,

"The Ramblings Of An Average Joe Stock Trader, 2nd Edition"

All of the Information I wish I knew in the beginning.

Copyright © 2011 Christopher L. Boyer
All rights reserved.
ISBN-13: 978-1460971505

Bonus Excerpt of
"Real Estate 101 Profit Max!!!"
101 Money Saving Ideas When Investing In Real Estate

Whether you are buying or selling a property, or you have never taken your first step. This bestselling book of ideas will help you get out there and make money. These are top, time tested tricks of the trade that will save you thousands upon thousands of dollars on every property. Stop taking risky gambles and start learning how truly successful real estate investor/flippers save on every move they make.

"Real Estate 101 Profit Max!!! is a coupon book of ideas."

1. Post office discount card. Before you buy anything from the big box hardware stores always stop buy the local post office and ask for a change of address form/packet. Inside the change of address packet is a coupon to Lowes for 10% off purchases up to $2000.00. Home Depot will honor the Lowes coupon. You also get this coupon in the mail a couple weeks after you move to a new address.

2. If you're going to hire a lot of the work out always make sure to hire the right people. People that have experience in doing the job. Make sure you get references and you actually call them.

3. Do repairs and improvements as if you were going to be the one living in the property.

4. Kitchens and bathrooms are the primary areas to spend the most money.

5. First impressions sell your house. Take everything into account. From the curb appeal to the way the house smells. View your house as if you are the buyer.

6. Take advantage of the big chain hardware stores match and beat by 10% policy.

7. If remodeling a kitchen and the cabinets aren't in too bad of shape, relocate them to the garage. Who doesn't love garage cabinets for storage?

8. Do it yourself experience will save you money. Spend a little time on each property learning something new.

9. Your first offer for a property should always be 30% or less off the asking price. If you're not embarrassed by your offer it's not low enough. All they can respond with is no.

10. Paint your front door red. Houses with front doors that are bright red typically sell faster. (color selection is regional, but the point is to make it loud and eye catching)

11. Houses that are listed and actually make it to the MLS (Multiple Listing Service) have already been picked through by real estate agents, their friends, clients, investors, and bank specialists. So don't be discouraged if you find it difficult to find a good deal straight off the MLS. Use the MLS as a guide. Find errors between the MLS, county tax office and the actual property. Appraisers that represent banks normally do a drive by appraisal and never step foot inside the property. Use their lack of thoroughness to your advantage. Some types of errors to look for

are; on file square footage not matching actual square footage, heated square footage errors, tax recorded number of bedrooms and bathrooms not matching property, etc.

12. Unless you are going to rent the property and have no plans to ever sell it, NEVER buy real estate to flip next to, or in the vicinity of apartment complexes or areas with high volumes of rental properties. The only exception is if you already have a buyer setup prior to you acquiring the property.

13. Join the local real estate investment club. If there isn't one in you immediate area consider starting one up. The contacts through the club potentially can save you money. But be cautious, many of the members of a long time existing club will prey on the new members trying to convince them that their bad apples are still good enough to eat.

14. You are not getting a good deal on a house if a new similar house across the street is selling for less. So many newbies think older is better. In reality most first time home buyers (especially the younger ones) will always lean towards the newer of the two.

15. When estimating what to price your property at or what to pay for a property check out all comparable (similar) sales of properties 1)in your neighborhood, 2)within a one mile radius, 3)within a three mile

radius. Use only the most recent sales dates. (not more than three to six months old)

16. Unless you are getting a ridiculously low price, or plan on renting the property, don't look at properties that have multiple foreclosures on the same street that are within sight of the primary property.

17. When reviewing the appraisal report on a property make sure to see if the appraiser addressed foreclosures in the vicinity. Foreclosures can have an impact on appraisal price. (especially if there is a large number of them in the area)

18. If you're stuck in a property and you are considerably upside down pay a professional to review the appraisal that was done when you first acquired the property. Many times appraisers don't put in much effort and manipulate property prices to please the bank or real estate agents. Appraisers are legally responsible for losses if they committed fraudulent acts. Consult an attorney.

19. Become an expert in calculating square footage. Many people don't realize there is more to measuring than length times width. Hidden corners and walls can really add up in lost square footage. Second floors and basements can become tricky areas. Errors in other people's measurements can lead to great profits (or losses) for you. If you find

calculating square footage a daunting task call a local appraisal company. Many appraisers offer a measuring service for very little money.

20. When calculating expenses always overestimate money going out, and underestimate money coming in. Practice this and you will never be disappointed.

Want to read more?

The remaining **eighty-one** ways can be found in the book,

"Real Estate 101 Profit Max!!!"
101 Money Saving Ideas When Investing In Real Estate

Copyright © 2011 Christopher L. Boyer

All rights reserved.

ISBN-13: 978-1466339811

ISBN-10: 1466339810

RECOMMENDED PUBLICATIONS, SHOWS, AND SITES

"The Instant Millionaire"
By Mark Fisher.

"The Millionaire Next Door: The Surprising Secrets of America's Wealthy"
By Thomas Stanley and William

"Short-Term Trading in the New Stock Market"
By Toni Turner

Day Trading Radio at www.daytradingradio.com

"Awaken the Giant Within: How to Take Immediate Control of Your Mental, Emotional, Physical and Financial Destiny!"
By Anthony Robbins

"The Courage to be Rich: Creating a Life of Material and Spiritual Abundance," and all books by Suze Orman and her television show, "The Suze Orman Show,"
www.suzeorman.com and
http://www.cnbc.com/id/15838523

"The Total Money Makeover: A Proven Plan for Financial Fitness," By Dave Ramsey www.daveramsey.com

"Fast Money" on CNBC
http://www.cnbc.com/id/15838499/

"Mad Money" with Jim Kramer on CNBC
http://www.cnbc.com/id/15838459/

"Real Estate 101 Profit Max!!!" by Christopher L. Boyer "Philips Phile" radio show on Real Radio104.1 and XM Extreme Talk 165, based out of Orlando Florida
http://www.realradio.fm/pages/phile.html

An abundance of information pertaining to everything statistical about America can be found on the US Census site http://www.census.gov/

"The Ramblings of an Average Joe Stock Trader, 2nd Edition," By Christopher L. Boyer

"Buy High, Sell Higher: Why Buy-And-Hold Is Dead and Other Investing Lessons from CNBC's The Liquidator" By Joe Terranova

"Schnitt Show" radio program on SiriusXM Extreme Talk 165 http://www.schnittshow.com

"The Secret"
By Rhonda Byrne

"The Information: A History, A Theory, A Flood"
By James Gleick

"The Black Swan: Second Edition: The Impact of the Highly Improbable"
By Nassim Nicholas Taleb

The Other Side of Zero

"Jump In Now"

The Question to Answer Index

Question	Page
What is the other side of zero?	1-9
Why is the other side of zero important?	5
Does this system work for anyone?	1-4, 11
Can the system work in any time frame?	6
Does this system work for someone making minimum wage?	11
What is step one?	14
What is step two?	14
How did I get myself into this debt?	15
What are the numbers for the calculations based on?	17, 33-34
What is the first thing I need to know?	18
What is the second thing I need to know?	18
What is the first thing I should do?	19
What if I don't know the exact amount of money I will be getting paid?	20

Why do you have a savings account?	21
Why should I get rid of the bank?	24
Do you have "Extra Money" and what should I do with it?	26
Is it possible to ever have "Extra Money"?	27
How do I account for unforeseen scenarios in life?	28
What about tax return money?	29
How much do I have if I you gave me $500?	30
What are the two types of interest?	31, 92-93
What is the system and how do I use the website?	32-47
What is an example of the system in use?	46
What if I have questions about the system?	48-50
What is a "Wash Event," or "Wash"?	49
What are some ways I can save money now?	51-70
Why is there an eight on the last page of this book?	63

How do I use the website to calculate what an expense will cost me over my lifetime?	70
How will those around me change as my life gets better financially?	71-73
How can I save when purchasing medical insurance?	75
How can I increase my daily income?	76
Should I relocate to a less expensive area?	78
What about bankruptcy?	78-81
Should I allow bills to be drafted from my account?	82
Why should I try to simplify my life?	83
Should I make paying my house off a priority?	84-85
What is pursuing my career dreams?	86
What if I am upside down financially on my house or my automobile?	86-87
How do I get a raise in pay if my employer won't give it to me?	87-88
What about retirement and social security?	89-90

What are "Unrealistic Numbers," and why should I get used to them?	90-91
What about taking a vacation?	91-92
Should I buy a used car or a new one?	94-95
Should I be making donations?	96-97
What if my wife or girlfriend does not want to stop using credit?	98-100
Should I find other people to talk to?	102
What if each time I try to get my accounts through a set amount I get knocked back down?	102-104
I am out of debt, now what?	105-107
What is critical mass and why is it important?	108-112
What if I want to learn more about stocks?	117-130
What if I want to learn more about real estate?	131-137
Do you recommend any other books, sites, or shows to help me learn quicker?	139-140

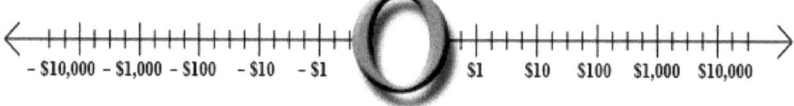

The Other Side of Zero

www.ingramcontent.com/pod-product-compliance
Lightning Source LLC
Chambersburg PA
CBHW071013200526
45171CB00007B/103